ARCHITECTURE OF CONSEQUENCE

DUTCH DESIGNS
ON THE FUTURE

Edited by Ole Bouman
NAi Publishers
Netherlands Architecture Institute

ISSUES:

FOOD 🍴

HEALTH 🌱

ENERGY 🔌

SPACE 🌐

TIME 🕐

SOCIAL COHESION 👫

VALUE CREATION €

ANSWERS:

Contact
**info@architecture
ofconsequence.nl**

Introduction
Ole Bouman

ARCHITEC-TURE OF CONSEQUENCE
Dutch Designs on the Future

When everything is proceeding smoothly, they are all dull and empty platitudes. 1: People need enough water and food: certainly. 2: They want to be healthy: I can see that. 3: They cannot manage without energy: logical. 4: They need to have sufficient room at their disposal: of course. 5: They also need enough time in their lives to manifest themselves: by all means. 6: And if a number of people are involved, it is important for them to be able to get on well together: that goes without saying. 7: If those people also want to trade with one another to reap the benefit of all those conditions, the books must balance: naturally.

CONJURE UP IMAGES OF THE CRISIS AND WHAT YOU SEE IS ARCHITECTURE.

Unfortunately, none of these conditions can be taken for granted at the moment. But then, we are not living in a peaceful era. We are dogged by one catastrophe after another. 1: Food chains are undermined. 2: Public health

is at risk. 3: Energy is running out. 4: The space is becoming cramped at many points. 5: The valuable time of our lives is slipping away. 6: Social cohesion is in decline. 7: And finally, we are increasingly coming to realize that for far too long we have been privatizing the gains and socializing the losses, resulting in an intense crisis of the economic system. In the meantime it has almost become a cliché to talk about the threat to the major planetary structures of subsistence. It would not take much for the catastrophe to become a dull platitude that we take for granted as well.

In this fraught period of multiple emergencies we are presenting a book about architecture. This may sound like a flippant diversion, a pause to contemplate the magnificence and reassurance of a beautiful building in an era that is growing more and more menacing. But the profession has no time for such relaxation as it is evident in retrospect that architecture has contributed mightily to a spread of global crises. If architecture is to demonstrate its added value, and to shed its burden of guilt, it needs better arguments than its ability to offer shelter.

Upon closer inspection that burden turns out to be massive. Conjure up images of the crisis and what you see is architecture: jammed roads, packed airports, automated transhipment centres, vast cowsheds, battery farms for pigs and chickens, meat factories, fast food outlets, shopping malls, hypermarkets and quarantine zones, worldwide material transportation, urban sprawl, condominium cities in the desert of Arizona, no-go areas and security walls, abandoned homes in ghost towns like Detroit or Sesena Nuevo. And it all started with design. But here the argument cuts both ways. Couldn't these images of the crisis until recently be considered as exemplars of the unprecedented success of globalization? And still. Think of an internationally acclaimed architect who is constantly jetting around the world, designing as many unique buildings as possible that in turn help generate an admiring mass tourism. Isn't this the one-off architecture that comes from far away to put the city on the world map? Hasn't this practice brought architects to a pinnacle of unparalleled fame? How can that pinnacle become an overnight symbol of cultural bankruptcy?

A PROFESSION THAT BASES ITS EFFORTS TO WIN CULTURAL RESPECT ON MERE SPECTACLE IS LIVING DANGEROUSLY.

The reason for this can only be found in the equally rapid awareness of the crisis. Architecture, design and construction are increasingly seen as part of the problem. The way in which this branch organizes and presents itself is now often taken to be a social debit – buildings that pay no heed to how they can be reached or accessed nor to what they contribute to society, how they can be adapted for use, the reduction of fossil fuel consumption, the provenance of their materials, the efficiency of the building process and their future management. Some people can already see the looming spectre of a totally irresponsible profession that seems bent on pricing itself out of the market, whatever the consequences. A profession that bases its efforts to win cultural respect on mere spectacle is living dangerously.

But the solution cannot dispense with architecture. The architect as sinner can only be redeemed by the architect as saviour, in the person of an architect who faces up to the challenge.

That is why this book is in particular about Dutch architecture. The Netherlands is in some respects harder hit than the average by the present crisis and will have to strive more than most other countries to find a solution. If this country ignores the challenge it will cease to exist. Without innovation the Netherlands is doomed to disappear as an independent country. Just look at the facts. The high population density has forced the Netherlands to become a leader in the industrialization of food production. The growing elderly population is a challenge to health care. Without a permanent supply of energy the country will be flooded. It needs new land to accommodate demographic pressure and to cater for changing lifestyles. It needs time to prove the value of innovations. It needs social peace to pursue its many desires. And as a crucible of capitalism, it is involved in and stands to gain more than any other country from a new benchmarking of the global economic system. If the Netherlands, under all this pressure, fails to think up something new, what is new will come up with something for the Netherlands.

The question now is whether Dutch architecture is up to the task. That is by no means a foregone conclusion. After all, the pressure just to keep plodding on is enormous. For example, a lot of energy in professional circles is still wasted on old feuds such as that between the modernists and the traditionalists, a controversy rooted in the notion that the essence of architecture is about style, external form, and that the architect therefore opts for the school to which he or she wants to belong, that of the modern era or that of providing 'what the customer wants'. This supposedly life-and-death struggle has been dragging on for most of a century by now.

A more recent notion is that a building can only be architecture if it is the embodiment of an intelligent concept, based on an extensive analysis of context, programme and the current architectural and philosophical debate. Didn't Dutch architecture become world famous with SuperDutch, the work of a generation that profiled itself with an unprecedented conceptual strength? This approach has certainly made a group of extremely intelligent designers famous, but it is debatable whether this is reason enough for architecture in general to

Trizidela do Vale,
Brazil, May 2009.

continue along the same lines in future.
Now, past mid-2009, it is doubtful whether the architectural profession in the Netherlands has enough resilience to turn the tide and seize new

THE ARCHITECT AS SINNER CAN ONLY BE REDEEMED BY THE ARCHITECT AS SAVIOUR, IN THE PERSON OF AN ARCHITECT WHO FACES UP TO THE CHALLENGE.

opportunities. According to a recent investigation by the Royal Institute of Dutch Architects (BNA), one third of the architectural firms have succumbed to the crisis in less than ten months, and the Chief Government Architect has announced an emergency programme to prevent the emergence of a lost generation as a result of the economic depression and the drastic cuts that are taking place in the building sector.
The architecture in this book has little in common with typical Dutch architecture in this sense, neither does it have any connection with an emergency programme. Its aim is nothing less than to be a radical part of the solution. This architecture presents solutions to questions that are both much larger than architecture and impossible to tackle without architecture. This architecture is not about the desired form or the possible analysis. It is above all about necessity, about architecture's capacity to resolve pressing problems. This architecture is not distracted by the current market situation, in which the question is whether there is work for architects. It is about a vision of the future and the focus that is required to keep that picture sharp. So it is also about the speculative minds of architects young and old which are essential for a vision of this kind and about their design research.
This book begins and ends beyond architecture, presenting a unique opportunity for architecture today, the rediscovery of a social necessity

that consistently produces worthwhile architecture. Such moments are historically rare. They occur only when the old procedures are no longer adequate and the new ones have not yet arrived on the scene. This crisis is too valuable an opportunity to let slip by, a chance to turn back to where architecture starts, in the creative spatial organisation of life – not in style choices or concept analyses, but in the identification of new spatial constellations; not in the spatial allocation and accommodation of a given programme, but in helping to create a spatial organization for multiple programmes; not in making things in space, but in organizing processes in time; in short, not in the object, but in performance. This architecture is not about superficial beauty, but about results. Eventually, architecture turns out to be an unparalleled field of innovation.

This insight probably comes as a surprise to the reader. Anyone who explores contemporary theories of innovation will soon notice that expectations about future social breakthroughs and thus future economic prosperity are mainly concentrated on high tech: information technology, biotechnology, nanotechnology and neurotechnology. In other words, bits, genes, atoms and neurons. That is where the vast resources for research are concentrated, where social relevance and social respect are located. Nobody in this global knowledge field is still betting on architecture – the profession of stones, soil, space and slowness. Nether is it logical to expect that breakthroughs in the technologies mentioned above will have immediate architectural outcomes as earlier technological revolutions did: the church, the palace, the factory, the station, the bank. How can architecture today benefit from progress in genetics and nanotechnology? Architecture is not just suffering from an economic crisis but also threatened by a crisis of motivation. If that lasts too long it will be faced with a crisis of talent too.

What can architecture do to avert this scenario and unite its social role in the present with its future mission? Simply put, it must start with what is necessary. More than any new technology the old technology of architecture provides solutions to problems associated with food chains, healthcare, energy flows, lack of space, time management, social tensions and the present economic system.
What is needed is a spatial organization that allows people to achieve self-sufficiency again, that constructs healthier environments, that

008

produces energy rather than merely consuming it, that does not cost space or time but creates them, that promotes cohesion, a spatial organization whose value is defined as a unified process of design, building and maintenance. This is an assignment with the appeal of an Apollo project, or, in the Dutch experience, the symbolic force of the Delta works project. Architecture has been presented with an opportunity that is seldom available.

An architecture that focuses on the many possibilities of intensification and combination is a realistic proposal. Rather than an architecture of monoprogrammatic zones, single issue spaces, zoning plans and highly individual, unrepeatable statements, it would be an architecture that derives sustainability from the

pact or movement in which all noses have to point in the same direction, but rather a competition in which the participants are driven by the same innovative motivation – their profession has set out to solve the problems it helped create. Visions of the future, images to lend force to that vision, strategies for getting there, the force of conviction to follow those strategies can all be found in this book. The only thing missing is effective implementation by decision makers. We hope that this book will help to find them.

THIS IS AN ASSIGNMENT WITH THE APPEAL OF AN APOLLO PROJECT, OR, IN THE DUTCH EXPERIENCE, THE SYMBOLIC FORCE OF THE DELTA WORKS PROJECT.

sharing of space, services, energy, transport, the public domain and of values, an architecture that through that sharing achieves wholly new typologies.

This book is full of examples of that kind of architecture, from CO_2-neutral to energy-producing buildings and landscapes, from high-quality architecture for lower income groups to a villa made from refuse, from temporary hotels in demolition zones to the redevelopment of existing social housing, from unique business alliances at the regional level to cooperative, productive teams involving local residents.

Architecture is already presenting this vision for the future, as this book demonstrates. The architects presented here, though often rivals in daily life, display a striking unanimity in their ambitions for their profession. Theirs is not a

FOOD

One person's waste is another person's food.

AMBURGERS   HOTDOGS

The depletion of natural resources, incursions on arable land, the overfishing of the seas, the shortage of fresh water – and in the future 9 billion mouths to be fed.

Preventive slaughter of cattle in connection with the risk of BSE infection, 1996.

🍴 **Industrial food production in the Netherlands is enormous and still growing, with a large energy requirement and high CO_2 emissions. Pumped full with hormones and antibiotics the welfare of farmed animals is subordinated and their physical condition often sacrificed to sate the vast demand for meat.**

Food production today leads to an increase of scale in architecture. More than 70 per cent of the land in the Netherlands is used for agrarian purposes. A mere half of its farming concerns account for 90 per cent of the county's food production. Supermarkets are growing ever larger all over the world. As a result of the industrialization of food production, ever less information is available about where our food comes from.

Two acres of wheat planned and harvested by the artist Agnes Denes on a landfill site in Manhattan's financial district, one block from Wall Street and the World Trade Center. (Wheatfield – A Confrontation: Battery Park Landfill, Downtown Manhattan – The Harvest, 1982.)

We need alternative food production chains. The ethics of the bio-industry, the energy wasted by global food distribution and sharply rising world food prices force us to think about new ideas for agriculture and livestock farming closer to home and even within the city.

Contact
**info@2012
architecten.nl**

Office
2012Architecten

RECYCLICITY

2012Architecten regards the city as a complex, changing and self-constructing environment in which feedback and reuse are necessary. Intelligent combinations of local processes of production and flows of residual materials lead to greater efficiency in each project and the emergence of a new aesthetic.

Themes

Villa Welpeloo is the first home that 2012Architecten have built following the Superuse method. About 60 per cent of the building materials come from the immediate surroundings of its location in Enschede. The textile industry that flourished here in the past has moved to the other side of the world, leaving the machinery to be sold off as scrap metal. In this way a continuous lift for thread can be used as a main support in construction. The secondary construction and the insulation materials have been taken from a small building. The façade cladding is made from the wooden cores of cable spools from a local cable factory. The building lift used for the construction now functions as a transport platform in the villa.

Photography:
Allard van der Hoek

Wikado

Wind turbines do generate sustainable energy, but the blades by with which the electricity is produced are made from material that cannot be reused and are written off after ten years; at the moment that means two hundred are scrapped each year. Five blades were sawn up to make towers and tunnels for a playground in Rotterdam. The stainless steel slides from the neglected playground were given a new place in the design.

Photography:
Allard van der Hoek

'The ideal conditions for a sustainable recycling society existed in the preindustrial era. Utilities and buildings were made from natural materials which could decay or be reused after a foreseeable period. The limitations of transport confined the distribution of material to within the local region and the costs of material in relation to labour were relatively high. Since in the last century practically all productive human activities were detached from one another and linked in a linear fashion, spatial planners now increasingly run up against conflicts between interest groups that exert only a negative influence on one another and are unable to benefit from one another's presence. It is high time for new cycles. The local production of food that is grown with the help of residual warmth from neighbouring industry and of which the residual material can be used in a biogas installation that provides fuel; or empty offices that are redesigned as homes, thereby reduce the housing shortage as well as bringing about a combination of functions in monofunctional urban districts.

By making these kinds of short circuits visible in the built environment, in the first ten years of its existence 2012Architecten has made a study of the potential of products that are categorized as waste. *Superuse* creates short circuits in the flows of materials by linking local demand and supply to one another, and building methods are developed that require minimal material processing. This procedure leads to a new aesthetic that appreciates the local presence alongside the use history of the applied product. The knowledge acquired is shared with other designers elsewhere in the world by means of a website, book and film.

To deploy *Superuse* on a larger scale, 2012Architecten is developing strategies and tools to attune the materials that become available to needs. Until the internet revolution, information about the nature and location of such materials was limited to the account books of its owner. Nowadays this information can be retrieved at any moment at any point in the world and combined as one chooses, opening up enormous possibilities in particular for materials that are in the wrong place at the wrong moment – the broadest definition of waste. A harvest chart is an example of a tool that provides insight into which materials are to be found in the environment of a building project. These are no longer the natural materials of the preindustrial era, but worn-out carpet tiles, frames from demolition sites, offcuts from factories, superfluous car windows, and superseded railway tracks. The knowledge now enables 2012Architecten to forge new links in designs.' – Jeroen Bergsma, Jan Jongert and Césare Peeren

IT'S IN THE MIX

Functional separation as a planning method has created monofunctional, isolated areas. 2by4-architects seek the solution to this problem in the addition of unexpected functions that make use of the available potential so that seemingly uninteresting spots become desired top locations.

Themes

Living right above industrial premises
The innovative construction of housing right on top of industrial estates takes advantage of a location already served by an infrastructure network, the existing green buffers or waterways that surround the site, the greater freedom of architectural expression and functional use inherent in such areas and their open character, and above all the ample space. The elemental concept of *living right above industrial premises* generates entirely new housing typologies with many diverse opportunities for working at home in an unusual setting. This one simple move would reverse the negative spiral of exodus, commuter sprawl, impoverishment and an unsafe environment and would immediately transform urban industrial locations into sustainable places to live.

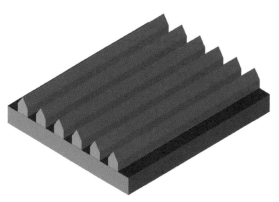

'The separation of functions that has taken place in the Netherlands in the last couple of decades has led to monofunctional zones. Take the industrial estates that have expanded to become dormitory towns without any form of city life, or the landscapes with a cultural-historical value that serve as inaccessible green buffers to stop cities from sprawling towards one another. Together with all the regulations and laws, which in the first instance seem to discourage any form of combined function, the separation of functions guarantees isolation and alienation.

The architectural practice of 2by4 involves research into architectural interventions which could produce an ideal mixture of functions for the upgrading of a monofunctional zone.'
– Remko Remijnse and Rocco Reukema

Boardwalk
A greater opportunity to access and enjoy the countryside of the Randstad would be an essential source of vitality and identity. The subtle intervention of the architecture of the *Boardwalk project* offers insights into scenic, natural and cultural-historical qualities. A hiking route is a new link in a system of connections which now makes it possible to walk all the way from the Green Heart of Holland to the North Sea, offering the experience of several landscapes along a single route.

1 coastal landscape
2 dune landscape
3 wooded landscape
4 closed polder
  landscape
5 water landscape
6 open polder landscape

Contact
mail@anneholtrop.nl

Office
Anne Holtrop

ENVIRON- MENTAL INSTALLATIONS

Anne Holtrop develops unique housing typologies primarily on the basis of the spatial circumstances that he encounters at a chosen location. The landscape is the guiding principle of the entire design process. He uses the internal organization of the homes to reinforce the exchange between private and public, which produces new ways of experiencing the immediate surroundings.

Thema

026

The *Trail House* (2009) has been designed for one of the few empty lots in the Dutch new town of Almere. Over the years spontaneous paths have emerged in the vegetation on this site because it is regular crossed by the people who live in the surrounding houses. The ground plan of the Trail House is integrally determined by the contour of part of this route. The existing paths indicate the direction of use. The different housing functions distinguish partly unwalled rooms. At the end of a blind corridor is a bath; further on the house is divided into a work area and a kitchen.

Photo: Bas Princen

The centre of the world, piled high and full of sediment. No one pushes his way through [...] But you sit at your window and imagine it, when evening comes.'
Franz Kafka

'It is futile, as Kafka wrote, to want to push one's way through to the problems of our time, to the centre of the world, to what is considered urgent or important. Architecture cannot be identified with solutions; architecture is not a visa to a country where utility holds sway. The two designs presented here issue a spatial statement which opens possibilities. Architecture sits at its window and tries to imagine itself – in order to approach the centre of its environment by constructing it.

The *Floating Gardens* and the *Trail House* are environmental installations in that they install environments that are both mental and physical. The architecture first provides windows, walls, thresholds and steps, creating the environment in which human activities and stories can take place. In these two projects the architecture stimulates the development of a life like no other. It makes the residents themselves pioneers in their new environment. We think of pioneers as belonging to an earlier era, but who can get through life without feeling a bit of a pioneer?

In the Floating Gardens design the water is a surface on which a floating environment can be constructed. The architecture presents the illusion that you can walk on the water. The houses are floating, inhabitable climbing frames for the landscape. The planted vegetation is discontinuous and rampant, the view of the surroundings is filtered by the gardens. Whoever lives here and looks out the window sees a water and vegetation which gratifies the human desire for a world that is visible and tangible.

In the Trail House the soil that has been covered by plants and shrubs has to be made accessible as a landscape after a house has been built on the well-trodden paths. Through the alignment of earlier paths the occupier inevitably becomes an element in the new landscape, an environment in which nobody has ever set foot before – and that in an artificial new town like Almere. The accessible parts of the environment become a house, and soon afterwards that same house makes an independent environment of what was previously untrodden.

In both cases, the house is seen as literally making the context accessible starting from scratch. Architecture is not the visa that has to be verified, but the barrier that brings a brief routine pause to the journey.' – Anne Holtrop (architecture) and Christophe van Gerrewey (text)

The *Floating Gardens* design (2008) envisages floating villas with facilities. A housing landscape is constructed in a lake. The homes are accessed by paths from the shore. The housing structures are clad with plants, trees and bushes which ensure that after a while they will completely disappear into their surroundings, while the surroundings can still be seen through the homes.

Office
ATELIER KEMPE THILL architects and planners

QUALITY SOCIAL HOUSING AS PRIME TASK

Based on the conviction that architecture need not be an elitist product but should be accessible for people with a low income, Atelier Kempe Thill aims at the optimization of social housing design. The result is high-quality architecture that no longer under-scores the distinction between high- and low-income classes.

Themes

The *Hiphouse* project in Zwolle gave studio Kempe Thill the opportunity to raise fundamental questions about the task of social housing. Within a tight budget, as is common in the Netherlands, a prototypical project could be implemented thanks to an ambitious client and the energetic support of the urban planners. A maximum of living quality was realized by radical minimization of the use of resources and consistent discussion of the building technology; maximum by minimum.

Photography: Ulrich Schwarz, Berlin

031

'In the past 25 years the design and construction of large-scale social housing has virtually disappeared from the political agendas of most highly developed Western countries and architects have shown less interest in designing such housing. The entire international avant-garde who became 'star architects' have actually driven the expectations surrounding architecture to a level that housing can never attain. This is both a social and an ethical problem. The architecture of housing must surely again become a key issue now that economic and environmental crises have arrived at our doorstep. Once again, Le Corbusier's statement of the 1920s, 'Architecture or revolution, the revolution can be avoided', will become particularly relevant.

Social housing has been one of the core activities of Atelier Kempe Thill since its establishment in 2000. The firm has always regarded the achievement of excellent quality within the tight budget of housing projects as a social necessity and an exciting challenge for architecture. Architecture should be accessible for all rather than for just a *happy few*. Social housing has traditionally been seen as cheap and shabby. It was a convention that social housing should not only be cheap but look it too. One of the primary aims of architects should be to overcome these preconceptions and to invest a maximum of quality and inspiration in social housing. This should be undertaken at the level of the building typology as well as in the choice of materials and the expressiveness of the building.

For Atelier Kempe Thill, housing design starts with the dwellings themselves: the aim is to give apartments an unexpectedly open, relaxed spatial layout that offers flexibility, generous views and a light interior with large windows for a contemporary life style. The apartment has become a *private landscape* with strong visual relationships with the outside, offering urban alternatives to suburban living. Due to the neo-liberalism of the past 15 years, *individuality* has come to be understood as *maximum individualism* or even *atomization*, a reflection of a society that has lost its coherence. If housing projects are given a strong collective dimension and expression, residents can share facilities and a collective identity that functions as a positive label. To achieve a strong design within a tight budget Atelier Kempe Thill has developed several strategies for achieving a maximum compactness combined with high-performance façades.

The architectural appearance of the buildings can be refined, especially given the large glass panes and generous sliding doors.' – André Kempe and Oliver Thill

HEALTH

The serious issue of ageing in the world's richest countries, the perpetual risk of epidemics as a result of globalization and universal mobility, an explosion of ailments such as Alzheimer's disease, obesity and diabetes.

The way we move through the city every day affects our health, and the Netherlands is no exception. The marked increase in allergies is the result of fine particles and contact with synthetic materials.

Many of today's health problems are connected with environmental planning. Cities are expanding at the expense of their green lungs, and valuable space for exercise close to home is disappearing. The loss is 'compensated' by substitute virtual worlds online and computer games.

The River Maas as a sports location. – Red Bull Cliff Diving, Rotterdam, 2009.

The definition of health is elastic, and so is the distinction between active and non-active. Medical breakthroughs can lead to spectacular changes in behaviour and in the way we perceive ourselves, but architecture has an unchanging mandate to provide a healthy environment to live in, no matter what the technological context may be.

Contact
info@biqstad.nl

Office
biq stadsontwerp

FROM SOCIAL ENGINEERING TO AVAIL- ABILITY

Instead of assessing existing buildings solely for their real estate value, biq stadsontwerp focuses on their value to society. With carefully chosen interventions the buildings are redeployed to better serve local social structures, contributing to sustainable urban renewal.

Themes

Redevelopment housing, Ommoord
In the Ommoord district, new households with a diversity of economic and ethnic backgrounds are not familiar with the sensitive codes of the locals. Reacting to this urbanization trend, a part of the brief can be translated into the design of communal traffic areas. We have taken a stake in diversification by introducing variation in the range of housing. Two buildings have been redeveloped as homes for the elderly with a care centre. Two other buildings have been divided up into independently functioning units with their own access. Ground-floor homes or first-floor homes accessed from the ground level have been added to all of the buildings.

Photography:
Stefan Müller, Berlin

043

'Today's architects were trained by the last generation that could envisage completing our world by means of an enormous planning machine capable of engineering the entire city from the top down. Belief in the feasibility of this programme has been whittled away in the Netherlands since the explosion of housing, by the sudden and unexpected overspilling of peripheral towns by the expanding Randstad, the rapid increase in mobility, and demographic shifts. All over Europe, such developments have had a profound effect on post-war housing districts, which were once the product par excellence of the idea of social engineering. There is no consensus in the Netherlands on the qualitative status of these districts. The village mentality of the Dutch post-war culture of reconstruction, once homogeneous and disciplined, has been lost and we are moving towards something new that does not have a clearly delineated form, but is at any rate heterogeneous, multicultural and globalized.

According to biq stadsontwerp, it is neither desirable nor feasible to demolish the post-war city and start all over again. It is not feasible simply because this part of the Randstad is so big. It provides two million homes. Nor is it desirable, since it ignores social themes such as sustainability, social cohesion and the increase in value of real estate. In the firm's experience the adaptive capacity of the post-war real estate available in the city is considerable. Moreover, existing social networks often prove exceptionally vital. It is therefore a mistake to assume that new structures must be imposed on post-war districts. The existing structures are generally orientated much more strongly towards dynamism and progress than towards a new status quo.

The name biq stadsontwerp (literally 'city design') makes it clear that the designers see their work as customized urban design based on the available urban material. They interpret new developments in the post-war city as urbanization processes rather than as interventions that are framed at a higher planning level and where the architect merely contributes the know-how. The search for different registers leads to a combination of targeted interventions that can produce a high yield from limited investments (know what, thus small messages) and long-term perspectives in which these interventions can find a place (know why, the prospects). The final picture is no longer the guiding factor in this process. This kind of urban design is built up layer by layer in the knowledge that further additions will follow in the future. The designs of biq stadsontwerp are assertive, but they do not seek out contrast. They are an active form of doing nothing.

While all this is pragmatically conceived, the question arises as to whether architecture can still avoid this pragmatism. The architecture of noncommittal impressions and the architecture of resistance will never be able to penetrate into the reality of the large building flows in the urbanized city. In pragmatic terms they produce mere ballast in the design process and are too much a part of the problem perceived by the evil outside world in which architecture nevertheless has to function. Architecture must once again engage with the political reality and become a part of the solution.' – Hans van der Heijden and Rick Wessels

TYPICALLY NL

For **CONCEPT0031** informal use of space is the primary starting point of the entire design process. After research by <mark>infiltration into local lifestyles</mark>, a programme is conceived that closely matches the common characteristics of local demand, bringing together people from different cultures.

Themes

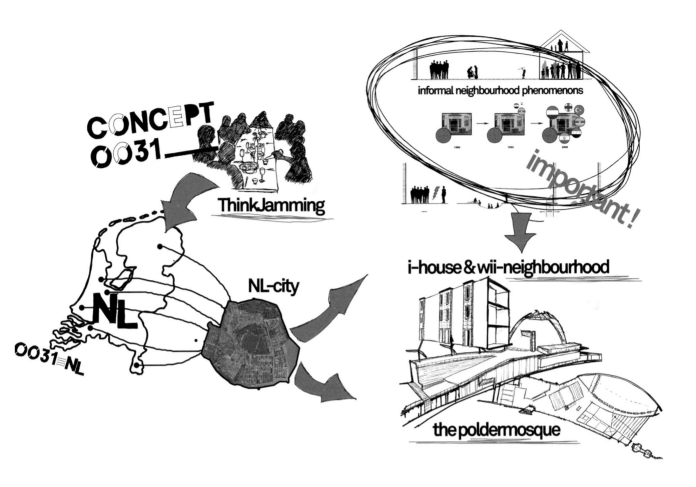

CONCEPT 0031

ThinkJamming

NL-city

NL

0031≡NL

informal neighbourhood phenomenons

important!

i-house & wii-neighbourhood

the poldermosque

NL-city – the perfect problem city composed of the existing problem districts in the Netherlands – is a physical new city that serves CONCEPT0031 as a test case for various investigations, designs, debates and denkjammz. Because they do not set out from the plural social structure, a false identity is created in urban development plans. The districts are unjustly rendered exotic and polarized. The informal inventory reveals how residents and visitors in the district deal with the private and the public domain. This brings out the difference between the formally planned district and the informally experienced district. A specific solution within this study are the club *Thirty-Seven* and the *Polder Mosque*.

The *Polder Mosque*, a spacious, open building with a grass roof and windmills, contains different functions, such as an elliptical area for prayer, a restaurant with lounge, a bazaar, office and class rooms, a grand café, an exhibition area, a party room and a Turkish bath. The aim is to provide a place of their own for the Muslims, often youngsters, who do not feel at home in the traditional mosques, as well as to appeal to other Muslims and non-Muslims through the variety of functions. These functions vary over time to cater for changing demands or requirements.

In cooperation with MEMAR.DUTCH

'Make a statement! Cool. ~~Right… with a presentation of the firm or of a project, or by writing a column?…~~ OK, how then?
By providing insight into the thought process that precedes writing the article that has been requested, I present the content of our work accompanied by some insight into the arguments and discussions in the firm. ~~After all, the work of an architect is not just the final thing that you see. It is the process, the complexity, the white noise, the failures, the inspirations, the discussions and the considerations within the total process that make the project what it is.~~ Yes!

For a long time 'the multicultural society' has been a concept people put into their mouths like chewing gum. They chewed and chewed until all the flavour had gone and then spat it out. ~~Understandable? Yes, because society leads to the wrong decisions if it is understood as a collection of people with different ethnicities. This legitimizes thinking in terms of compartments, and levels out different unique identities.~~ But society is more than classification by ethnic background – the pluricultural society is categorized by age, health, sexual preference, dress style, standard of living, music style… That is 'the pluricultural society'!

Instead of whitewashing society, architecture should provide scope for the dynamism of the pluriform society. In doing so, the architect should give the client not what he asks for but what he wants. There's an essential difference! The client doesn't always know… ~~But do we always know, then? Hmm…~~ YES! We have to convince; we are the trained specialists and we have grown up in different cultures, among different religions, risen from the street to eventually become representatives of Dutch architecture. ~~Proud!~~

So… where do the solutions lie? ~~Assume responsibility!~~ Every design has to be a combination of a vision of society, programmatic demands and visual expression. We want our work to be critical above all else, to provoke reactions and to involve people. ~~After all, you don't just make a design…~~ How do we achieve this? The results of the 'denkjammz' – meetings in which committed people from different backgrounds discuss all kinds of social issues in an informal setting – form the basis for the follow-up designs, debates or publications. ~~Political, economic, religious and social contradictions become clearer – the field of tension in which an architect continually moves.~~

In charting the pluricultural reality, it turns out to involve not only the district that is planned but the district that is experienced. ~~Issues and processes in the private, public and commercial spheres are characteristic that are not immediately visible and often have an informal character.~~ An inventory of informal facilities and activities offers an interesting new perspective on everyday reality in the city and thereby on the real context of the pluricultural society. ~~By moving about in a district or city without prior assumptions and adapting to the local language and codes, an underlying dimension of people, relations and activities is opened up.~~

Our projects show what is special about how we work. ~~The gay club, the mosque, the refugee centre, the disadvantaged neighbourhood… What shall I show? We have examples from the Polder Mosque to the recently completed open-minded Thirty Seven club, which is open to a broader public and where both homosexuals and heterosexuals can meet one another. Damn…~~ They range from a mosque to a gay club, which is typically Dutch and typically concept 0031.' – Ergün Erkoçu

Contact
**info@dezwarte
hond.nl**

Office
De Zwarte Hond

DUTCH REALISM

De Zwarte Hond is convinced that only building takes the profession further. The real transformation process does not get under way until after implementation. Buildings by De Zwarte Hond offer specific design solutions for today while deliberately leaving room for manoeuvre so that they can be put to a different use at some time in the future.

Themes

The Blue City, East Groningen
With the construction of a lake with a surface area of 800 hectares and 700 hectares of vegetation, plus the implementation of five unusual residential environments, new opportunities are offered to the sparsely populated area of East Groningen. Making the landscape suitable for recreation and enjoyment of the natural scenery means the local economy can obtain new sources of income. These kinds of large-scale transformations are in themselves an investment in an area that creates jobs, and the transformation of agricultural land into a lake and greenery creates opportunities for the development of new, high-quality housing environments. These housing environments attract new residents and will encourage businesses to relocate to the area as well.

Photo top: Dagblad van het Noorden

Photo bottom: De Groene Zoden

'Every implemented project design makes a cultural, social and economic impact, whether in urban design, landscaping or architecture, is as an engine for development. Plans are non-committal. Anyone who wants to change anything has to implement something.

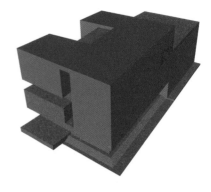

Each De Zwarte Hond design is an attempt to reinforce and facilitate the spatial and social cohesion. De Zwarte Hond produces buildings and urban designs free of iconography, so that they will always allow appropriation by the context and by their users.

Cooperation with all the participants plus alliances with parties who have specific knowledge are crucial instruments for De Zwarte Hond. That is why the firm facilitates this network and why it functions as a design platform. The firm constantly and objectively investigates all of the circumstances and limiting conditions and weighs up the consequences, so that its design will be based on a broad, unprejudiced outlook without being orientated to sectoral interests. It is a condition of this approach that as architects or urban designers we are not preoccupied with a final image, style or signature, but are open to genuine consultation. Only then can a joint

Ronald McDonald House, Groningen
The building fits naturally into the neighbourhood but raises its context to a higher plane through the use of materials, complexity and details. For this temporary community of parents in a vulnerable position it was important to avoid an institutional atmosphere and to opt for a spatial organization that would encourage but not insist upon mutual support and solidarity. The implicit programme was so designed that there is ample opportunity for chance encounters between the residents, while there are still places everywhere to which they can retreat.

Photography:
Jeroen Musch

result arise, resulting in a design without an individual author, without representation but with a clear contextual identity. This only works if the designer feels responsible for the entire process and operates with an open attitude. To create new spatial and social cohesion, each project has to offer possibilities that are not specifically circumscribed or defined. De Zwarte Hond therefore carefully charts programme, context, technique and budget so that opportunities arise for the economic use of the space. This leaves room for an implicit programme and use in the space between the requested programme and the intelligent explicit translation. A building or urban plan is a motivated interpretation within the parameters of the assignment. The undefined space within it initiates collectivity and social cohesion and creates conditions for planned and unplanned developments.

The experience of De Zwarte Hond is that, particularly in a complex socio-economic context, certain tendencies can only be tackled by implementing designs. At most, plans can only put issues on the agenda or indicate directions towards solutions, but the design itself cannot stimulate any change. Actual creation in a difficult environment calls for resilience and resolute craftsmanship. The designer is the conscience of the entire trajectory from formulation of the brief to implementation. Unconditional dedication to the design goes without saying, but a designer should also assume responsibility for its implementation.'
– Jurjen van der Meer, Willem Hein Schenk, Jeroen de Willigen and Eric van Keulen

Office
Doepel Strijkers Architects

ADAPT OR DIE

Doepel Strijkers Architects anticipates the effects of climate change by closing various cycles at the building level. The upscaling of this strategy to the level of cities and even countries is the next step. The logic of flows, paying attention to social, cultural and practical aspects ensures a balanced final result.

Themes

Photo: J. Koelewijn,
Spiegelkubus Bonnet,
1992-2008 Rotterdam.

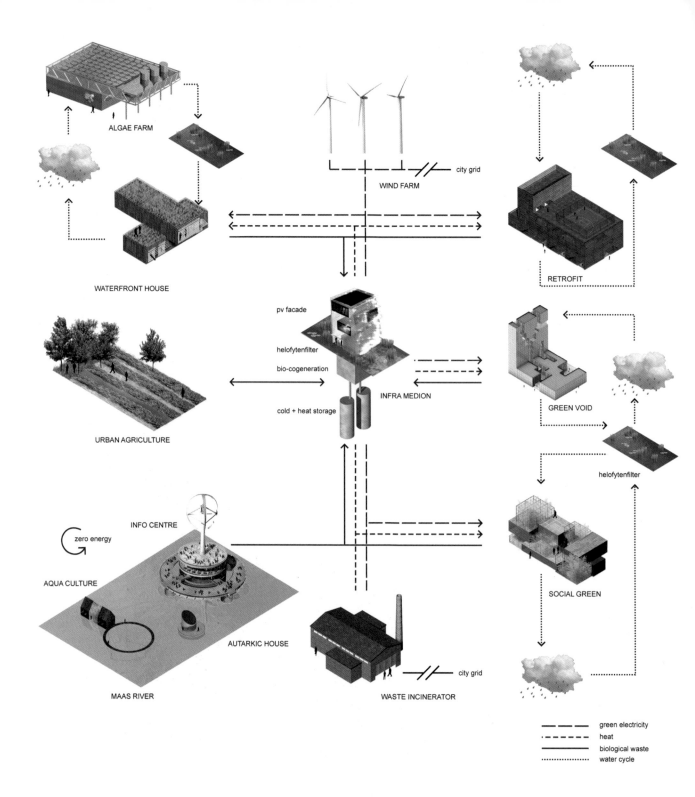

ALGAE FARM

WATERFRONT HOUSE

URBAN AGRICULTURE

INFO CENTRE

zero energy

AQUA CULTURE

AUTARKIC HOUSE

MAAS RIVER

WIND FARM

city grid

pv facade

helofytenfilter

bio-cogeneration

cold + heat storage

INFRA MEDION

WASTE INCINERATOR

city grid

RETROFIT

GREEN VOID

helofytenfilter

SOCIAL GREEN

green electricity
heat
biological waste
water cycle

'It is no longer sufficient to focus purely on architecture and strategies for preventing climate change. It is essential that we develop cities that can adapt to the effects of global warming, especially in low-lying areas like the Netherlands and in the developing countries which will be hardest hit. The time has come. Climate change and the global economic crisis have created the conditions for a renewables revolution. The coming decades will see a shift from an economy driven by fossil fuel to one based on renewable energy, a transition that will be accompanied by innovative architectural typologies and urban forms, derived from a new logic, the logic of energy flows and decentralized production.

Nature works in cycles. We can mimic this in the built environment, thereby optimizing the use of energy, water and natural resources. This principle is applied in *REAP* (Rotterdam Energy Approach and Planning), a methodology developed for CO_2-neutral city design.[1] The first step is to reduce the amount of energy a building consumes. Considering that 98 per cent of the built environment is existing stock, there are huge gains to be had by *retrofitting*. Smart design of new structures based on simple, age-old principles such as orientation to the sun and wind, compact volumes and good insulation can immediately reduce the energy demand by up to 40 per cent.
The second step is to balance energy demand and supply on the building scale. Strategies include harvesting heat from waste streams and energy exchange between functions. If a balance cannot be created at the level of the building, we upscale to the cluster or district level. By harvesting available energy and putting it back into the system or utilizing it at a higher level, we can eliminate waste altogether. Energy, water and materials stay in either the biological or the technical cycle. The final step in this approach is the generation of renewable energy at both the building and district levels. It is already technically possible to create buildings and districts that generate more energy than they consume, making the step towards decentralized production a reality.

This methodology results in urban configurations and buildings with an inherent logic based on flows. Form is not preconceived or image-driven. It is a logical response to climatic parameters, available technologies, local materials and energy flows. But the design of a building or the transformation of a district is not just about energy, water and waste. The process itself needs to be given form if it is to have an added value for the community and local economy. There is little point in an energy-neutral building or district if you are not concerned with its social function, cultural significance or long-term use. This is the element that closes the circle.' – Duzan Doepel and Eline Strijkers

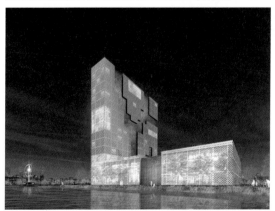

Stadshavens Rotterdam 1600 ha The Rotterdam Climate Campus was launched in November 2008 to transform the *Stadshavens Rotterdam 1600 ha* (City-Ports Rotterdam 1600 ha) from a fossil-based to a renewable economy.[2] The ultimate ambition is to achieve a sustainable harbour intrinsically connected with the surrounding city and characterised by a high in ecological, social and sustainable quality of life. A sustainability standard calculated from ten qualitative and quantitative indicators forms the basic set of criteria for all developments in the region.[3] The synergy between innovation and district development will make the Rotterdam Climate Campus, CityPorts Rotterdam and the Delft-Rotterdam region the locus of innovation and knowledge generation in north-western Europe.[4]

[1] *REAP* (Rotterdam Energy Approach and Planning) developed in collaboration with Delft University of Technology, JA, and the Municipality of Rotterdam, commissioned by the Rotterdam Climate Initiative and CityPorts Rotterdam.

[2] The Dutch Clean Tech Delta is a public-private partnership between the Municipality of Rotterdam, the Port of Rotterdam, the business sector and knowledge institutes.

[3] Sustainability Standard CityPorts Rotterdam 1600 ha. Developed in collaboration with Nico Tillie (Delft University of Technology) and Professor Jan Rotmans (Drift, Erasmus University).

[4] Based on the Rotterdam Climate Campus conceptual business case 'From Climate Campus to Clean Tech Delta'.

ENERGY

JCDecaux

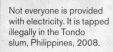
Not everyone is provided with electricity. It is tapped illegally in the Tondo slum, Philippines, 2008.

More human activities than ever putting pressure on finite sources of energy have created a need for an Apollo project for alternative energy production. The battle for energy is in full swing.

The Netherlands consumes a lot of energy. Reduction is fraught with difficulties. For instance, the country is only kept dry thanks to permanent pumping, and it depends to a large extent on hothouse food production to maintain its export balance. Energy management across the entire social system must be scrutinized and subsequently changed.

IKEA

ess First

om 37
ds Kolk 15

 **For many years energy has been a secondary factor in architectural design, and it does not yet occupy a prominent place in the syllabus of architecture courses. The consequences of this approach are calculable in our carbon footprint.**

JCDecaux

Energy is the engine of civilization. The need to find a new energy regime is a challenge to humankind on every level from the global to the individual.

Contact
info@jankonings.nl

Office
Jan Konings

AN ANIMATED PUBLIC DOMAIN

The temporary projects of Jan Konings show the <mark>potential of areas in transformation</mark>. Instead of going through a functionless interim phase, Konings' interventions free up such areas to offer unique possibilities for their use. Past and present are linked, and even before the implementation of the new plan the image delivers a positive impulse.

Themes

Hotel Transvaal fills the intermediate space that has been created as a result of the large-scale transformation of the Transvaal district of The Hague. Empty homes and new flats that have not yet been sold are fitted out as 1 to 5-star hotel rooms. When the apartments have been sold or the buildings slated for demolition have actually been knocked down, the hotel rooms are relocated. Hotel Transvaal makes use of the existing amenities of the neighbourhood. Within walking distance you can find a dry cleaner, hairdresser, launderette, baker, beauty and massage salon, bath house, conference room, bar, nightclub, internet café, call centre, swimming pool, tennis court, fitness centre, snack bar and restaurant. A central tobacconist's shop acts as the reception area.

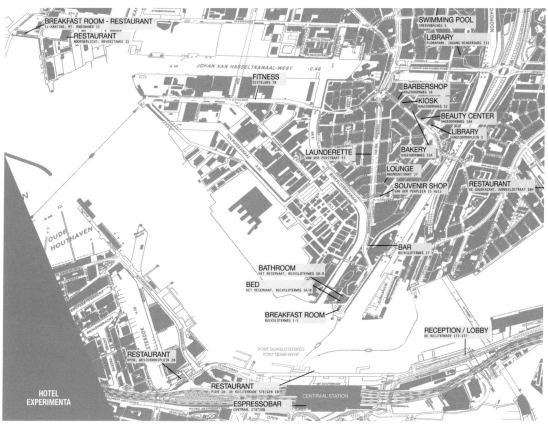

Hotel Experimenta – a lightweight object, made of foam and easy to transport – is a temporary hotel on the northern bank of the IJ waterway in Amsterdam with a single room with a double bed and a view. The other facilities and services are found at other locations. The neighbourhood as a whole forms the hotel, the streets are the hotel corridors, and the residents are the hotel staff, each with his or her own specialization. You have to go out of doors for breakfast or to use the toilet, washbasin and bath, television, restaurant or sauna. The ground plan of the hotel shows where the facilities and services are located. Depending on what the residents have to offer, this changes every day. Moreover, each new location has its own special features and local possibilities, so that the physical appearance of the hotel will be continually changing.

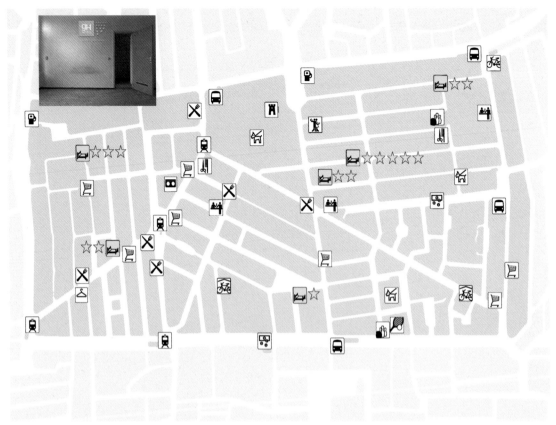

'The public domain is at risk. It is becoming increasingly regulated and privatized, while at the same time becoming increasingly dysfunctional. It is a storage cupboard for the programme that is considered necessary, in which more importance is attached to drainage, cables and pipes, parking lots, pavements, roads, traffic signs, speed ramps, anti-parking bollards, informal meeting places and dog toilets than to the public domain as such. Everything is perfectly organized, everything has been taken into account, and nothing can happen. Public life is something that happens elsewhere, sometimes even indoors.

The planned and controlled world of the public domain resembles that of the theme park. Visitors to the Efteling, the fairy-tale theme park in the south of the Netherlands, spend all day looking for paper, plastic, empty bottles and other rubbish. They enjoy putting the waste they have found into the mouth of the Paper Gobbler, a gnome with a fat belly who repeats the recorded message 'Paper here, paper here…' Masses of people take part in this voluntary form of public participation. The park is always clean and tidy. In the Efteling this is called an infill attraction. Infill attractions appear to be insignificant and gratuitous additions between the main attractions that grab most attention in the theme park, but they turn out to be essential links in providing cohesion for the whole. They are excellent cohesive elements.

The artificial world of the Efteling theme park seems to function well. Unlike the regulated public domain, the Efteling is animated; the public is encouraged to take an active part. The public domain is reinvented in this completely private environment and infill attractions are crucial in that process. The addition of infill attractions to the public domain makes it possible to create moments and places of seduction and activation within the demands of efficiency and planning. It is there that a link is forged between different publics, between the public and the object, and between the public and its immediate surroundings. Infill attractions create the conditions that can give rise to a new public domain.' – Jan Konings

Stay is a photo project about the different ways in which people stay in Rotterdam

Photo top:
Museum Park bridge

Photo bottom:
Merwehaven detention boat, 288 beds for illegal immigrants

In cooperation with Ralph Kämena

Contact
info@freehouse.nl

Collaboration

Freehouse
(Jeanne van Heeswijk & Dennis Kaspori)

RADICALIZE LOCAL PRODUCTION

The principle of reciprocity is decisive in the Freehouse concept of Jeanne van Heeswijk and Dennis Kaspori. Cooperative teams involving residents, entrepreneurs and educational institutions within the boundaries of a neighbourhood lead to a different kind of entrepreneurship with new products, services and hands-on training facilities. These coproductions promote economic self-sufficiency and cultural self-awareness, contributing to the social cohesion of an area.

Themes

DE MARKT VAN MORGEN
ZONDAG
7 JUNI 2009

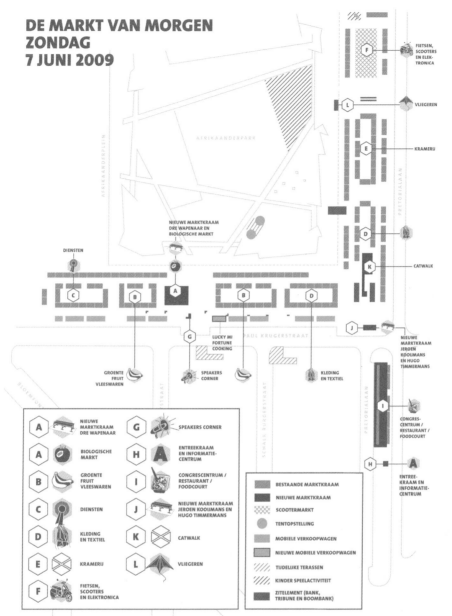

Afrikaander Market
The Afrikaander district will undergo a major transformation in the years ahead. The nearby construction of two housing estates of middle class homes will alter the social and economic composition of the population of the whole Feijenoord district. In 2008-2009 the Freehouse model was applied in Rotterdam-South to give a boost to the Afrikaander district so that the people who live there could share in the economic benefits of the redevelopment.

A scale 1:1 model as manifesto
A detailed live sketch of the ideal market of the future, devoting more attention to goods and services, cultural expressions, new market stalls and a renewed market organization as well as a considerable rearrangement of the available space.

A	NIEUWE MARKTKRAAM DRE WAPENAAR	G	SPEAKERS CORNER	
A	BIOLOGISCHE MARKT	H	ENTREEKRAAM EN INFORMATIE-CENTRUM	
B	GROENTE FRUIT VLEESWAREN	I	CONGRESCENTRUM / RESTAURANT / FOODCOURT	
C	DIENSTEN	J	NIEUWE MARKTKRAAM JEROEN KOOIJMANS EN HUGO TIMMERMANS	
D	KLEDING EN TEXTIEL	K	CATWALK	
E	KRAMERIJ	L	VLIEGEREN	
F	FIETSEN, SCOOTERS EN ELEKTRONICA			

	BESTAANDE MARKTKRAAM
	NIEUWE MARKTKRAAM
	SCOOTERMARKT
	TENTOPSTELLING
	MOBIELE VERKOOPWAGEN
	NIEUWE MOBIELE VERKOOPWAGEN
	TIJDELIJKE TERASSEN
	KINDER SPEELACTIVITEIT
	ZITELEMENT (BANK, TRIBUNE EN BOOMBANK)

Branch selection: Themed areas were introduced to expand the range, to achieve a quality balance and to trim back on the market glut of cheap textiles and vegetables. The themed areas mean extra attention can be paid to the linking of products, related services and functions.

Market assortment: The one-sided assortment was expanded with higher quality products within the existing stalls and new stalls with biological products.

Presentation: An attractive presentation of products leads to increased sales. During 'Tomorrow's Market' extra attention was paid to improved presentation on a stall, encouraged by using the expertise of stylists and designers.

Local production: The designer Cindy van den Bremen and women in local sewing and handicraft groups make clothing and accessories using fabric and haberdashery supplied by the Afrikaander Market. These 'Suit Yourself' products are sold at a Freehouse stall run by the women themselves. The food designer Debra Solomon and local catering entrepreneurs are developing a collective local restaurant with an international menu. The ingredients for 'Lucky Mi Fortune Cooking' are bought locally and local entrepreneurs are challenged to use their skills to expand the range, from the production of ginger beer to a Turkish deep fried meat snack.

New market stalls: To enhance the presentation and retail opportunities, Dré Wapenaar and Jeroen Kooijmans/Hugo Timmermans designed new prototypes of market stalls that will influence the future organization of the market. The stalls can be opened and closed and combined to form, for example, a roofed terrace.

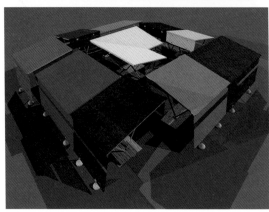
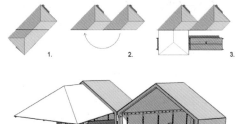
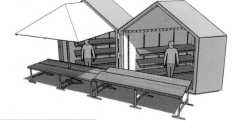

'Freehouse creates space, both literally and metaphorically, for encounters between local entrepreneurs, young people, local residents, artists and designers to exchange knowledge, experience and ideas. The linking of economic and cultural capital in a form of co-production reinforces the economic position of the parties involved and makes visible the cultural process of devising and implementing new products.

'Free House', or 'Freihaus', a model with medieval origins, offered space to groups of outsiders active in alternative economies, people ill-disposed to conventional means of political and social participation. The contemporary form of this model recognizes the positive contribution of others to public space and local culture, but it concentrates on a locally-orientated approach. The result of local cooperation can be seen in the openness of public cultural production that in turn becomes a driving force for change in the locality.

The Afrikaander Market, whose 300 or so stalls offer the most exotic range of produce to be found in Rotterdam, has been in decline for several years; turnover is falling, range is decreasing and market traders are increasingly

staying away. To accentuate the culturally diverse and small-scale character which distinguishes the Afrikaander district and its market from the surrounding districts, Freehouse and Kosmopolis Rotterdam involved entrepreneurs, residents, market traders, cultural producers, social service organizations and policy makers in various co-productions in the field of cultural entrepreneurship. The needs, wishes and insights of all the stakeholders and the different forms of capital (economic, social and cultural) in the district were made visible each week by means of a series of small-scale interventions in which possible innovations could be tested.

As these initiatives were being realized it became clear that it was high time for a radical review of the policy and regulations that apply to the markets in Rotterdam. For instance, at the moment it is not possible to combine products and services on the same stall, meaning that production processes important for the district, such as a sewing and repair service at a clothes stall or the preparation and consumption of food on location in a food court with a terrace is forbidden in the market.

Knowledge trajectories and production workshops were set up to stimulate local cultural cooperation to bring local production to the market. Entrepreneurs from around the Afrikaanderplein were challenged to take a more active part in the development to help make the market a network hub for local small-scale retailers.' – Jeanne van Heeswijk and Dennis Kaspori

Amenities and services: Co-productions of amenities and/or services in combination with products were given tangible form in, for example, a demonstration of headscarf knots by a group of women entrepreneurs at a stall selling scarves. A sewing and repair service was added to a second-hand clothes stall.

Meeting platforms: The red carpet was used for fashion shows with items available on the market, and for clothes designed by young local designers such as the Modehippies and Roffa 5314. The market cryer Lennart Pieters expressed his positive expectations for the future while the stand staff offered unusual products and everyone was invited to present ideas about the district.

Contact
mail@must.nl

Office
Must urbanism

MUST MAKES THE CITY

For Must urbanism the design starts with the active involvement of all the parties who have a share in the design and building process to arrive at a joint formulation of the assignment. The firm maintains supervision as far as possible from the initial stage down to completion to ensure that the basis of support is guaranteed throughout the entire process. Only then can the design be a logical consequence of the coalitions formed.

Themes

The most direct relation between urban design and the interested parties arises in projects where individual residents can have a home for their own personal use. Urban development on the basis of private commissions is thus one of the areas in which Must urbanism develops specific knowledge implementing the result in various roles and projects.

1 *Almere Overmaat* is an itemizing design study of the urban planning conditions for the development of a city of 25,000 homes on the basis of private commissions. The plan shows that a substantial part of the town of Almere can be realized by its own residents. The results of this study were incorporated in the housing programme drawn up in 2007 entitled 'I build my house in Almere'.

1

'The Netherlands is made up of coalitions. Canals, polders, railway tracks and city expansions are the result of temporary alliances between bankers, entrepreneurs, administrators, engineers and the generous Royal Family. Space has become a scarce commodity in the Netherlands. Environmental planning is always a conflict between pension funds, project developers, government bodies, NGOs and a thousand and one interest groups over the use of land. The everyday practice of Must urbanism shows that in this arena it is still possible to form alliances with parties with different agendas and to implement complex projects, producing urban design by means of temporary coalitions.

The coalition urban design of Must is based on the premise that environmental planning is the terrain of parties that take the initiative, such as professional principals, residents, interest groups or Must itself. They select their allies each time depending on the goal they want to achieve. In today's diverse society the idea of a single, comprehensive final objective is untenable. Coalition urban design involves consensus on projects. The shifting composition of the coalitions determines the dynamism of the spatial order.

To guarantee the quality of the city and the right conditions for its own design projects the firm works on itemized recommendations and projects that lead to the formulation of a brief. The knowledge that Must has built up in the process concerning space and infrastructure, water, culture, shrinkage, urban restructuring and working with private commissions puts it at a significant advantage. Must directly links knowledge at the administrative and strategic levels with the level of the project to be implemented, and vice versa. This smooth traffic between projects and positions is the overarching and crucial project that links all the projects. Knowledge is a thread running through the different projects, assignments, scale levels and territories.

In the Must methodology, observation, interpretation and implementation are linked in changing sequences. Perception precedes all else. Phenomenology has pride of place, supplemented with knowledge of the patterns of the residents and users. Must remains an open source. Sources are not withheld and all information is shared. Cartography, an important step in the formulation of assignments provides insight for third parties into spatial structures and the related force fields.

The interpretation of the brief is a matter of getting the needs of the interested parties into clear focus. Must employs design research to present possible solutions on different scale levels, broken down into fixed components and organized in a matrix of options. Discussion of the matrix exposes agendas and provides a clear picture of the direction of a broadly shared solution at the strategic, political and everyday level. The parties jointly construct an urban design that can stand up for itself in the complex force field of environmental planning.

Must commits itself to the design and to a measured process of implementation. Through its permanent involvement, all the way through to the actual implementation, it is possible to guarantee the qualities of every plan right down to the level of fine detail. Many designs can fit together seamlessly. Urban design lays down structures that will ideally last for generations. Autonomous statements contribute only by rare exception. Must prefers to cause an invisible mutation of the urban fabric that comes to life immediately.' – Robert Broesi, Pieter Jannink, Wouter Veldhuis

2

2 *Houses in Haarlem*
Must has taken the initiative to develop two private homes on a plot of land in Haarlem that had become vacant. The homes, designed by Border Architecture, have a spectacular spatial organisation that could never be built by a regular developer. Yet the contemporary homes fit perfectly into the look of the nineteenth-century street. By 2009, the wound from a couple of years earlier had healed.

Photo: Jeroen Musch, 2009

3 The urban development plan for the *Landhof* district in Eindhoven provides the spatial frameworks for 250 homes that will be built by collectives of residents. The plan offers a robust landscape framework within which the collectives are given the scope to build their own homes and to execute specific communal amenities. The first four collectives are working on the design of their homes under the supervision of Must and the local authority. Construction will commence in 2010.

4 The research project called *the Private City* has been initiated by Must in ten districts in the Netherlands built as private commissions. The research yields knowledge about the critical factors for a successful urban development plan carried out by individuals. The report will appear at the end of 2009.

3

rieteiland - amsterdam   waterrijk - woerden

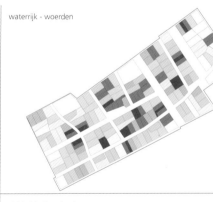

skoatterwald - heerenveen   stripheldenbuurt - almere

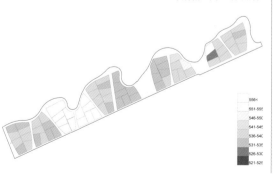

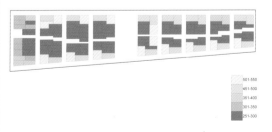

4

HARVESTING SPACE

Reducing the use of raw materials and energy is not enough to counteract climate change. The architecture of MVRDV offers alternatives to compensate for the negative consequences of our consumer behaviour. **Multiple use of space, energy and other resources** must lead to a net gain rather than merely a reduction of waste.

Themes

1 *KM3, the Cube*, is a study of the compact city (2000-2005). Based on Dutch statistics, the study visualizes the spatial needs of one million people. A cube of 3.37 kilometres contains all the programme required, including the necessary buffers around industries. Housing and offices occupy less space than expected; 20 per cent of the cube's space is reserved for food production and 45 per cent for oxygen. This study emphasizes the need to work on these domains, which have been so badly neglected by the architectural and urban traditions.

Project KM3: MVRDV / Berlage Institute / Wieland & Gouwens

1

'At some point in the nineteenth century we lost our 'CO$_2$ innocence', as the German philosopher Peter Sloterdijk recently put it. Nobody today argues against the need to be more efficient and productive in, for example, land use. Since we consume too much anyway, we have to decide either to reduce consumption, or to use the earth's surface in a more efficient way, which could be thought of as farming. Instead of merely consuming less, we can still have more. The Dutch are used to creating land (polders) and to being highly productive per square metre, but we still have not reached the limits of researching how combined functions can be transformed into integrated designs in which buildings produce cycles within themselves.

Recently more and more neighbourhoods have been designed to produce their own energy by integrating renewable energy devices such as solar panels, solar boilers and wind turbines which are placed on the rooftops or on public land. Water recycling and purification can be integrated, though this sometimes requires a large amount of space. If, however, the occupants are made aware of what it takes to produce clean water the effect is eye-opening. These neighbourhoods sometimes become so effective that they even start their own company to sell off the surplus energy they have generated.

It would be interesting to see if we can broaden the profession of architects and urban designers from creating culturally and functionally efficacious designs to making productive designs as well. Some of these aspects could be simply translated into briefs and, if necessary, into budgets, but it becomes even more interesting if the desired productivity can be associated with the design – agricultural aspects, the lives of plants and animals (*Pig City*), floating cities, or by using energy produced by humans themselves through their body heat, movements and activity.

The goal is to develop smart contemporary designs which allow the multiple use of resources, space included. Through radical, methodical research and the use of the complex bodies of data that result from the way we live, the contemporary design process can lead to integrated designs that offer solutions to the issues raised in this publication.' – Winy Maas, Jacob van Rijs en Nathalie de Vries

2

3

4 *Pig City*
The Netherlands is the largest exporter of pig meat in the EU. Transforming the sector into organic farming would result in 75 per cent of the country's surface area being dedicated to pig meat production. *Pig City* (Port of Rotterdam, the Netherlands) is a tower of 40 stacked organic pig farms, one abattoir, and related in-house energy and food production that would solve many issues in the bio-industry, among them cruelty to animals and the use of space for farming, transport, energy generation and animal feed production.

5 In the *Eco-City Montecorvo* (Logrono, Spain, 2008 – 2014) only 10 per cent of the 56 hectare site is taken up by the 3,000 social housing units and public facilities which meander as stacked volumes over the site, offering panoramic views and leaving room on site for the production of energy, water collection and water purification. This energy park is designed for recreation and energy production; representing a new typology of public space which saves the emission of 6,000 tonnes of CO_2 per year. An on-site research centre and museum will collect and disseminate knowledge about renewable energy.

4

5

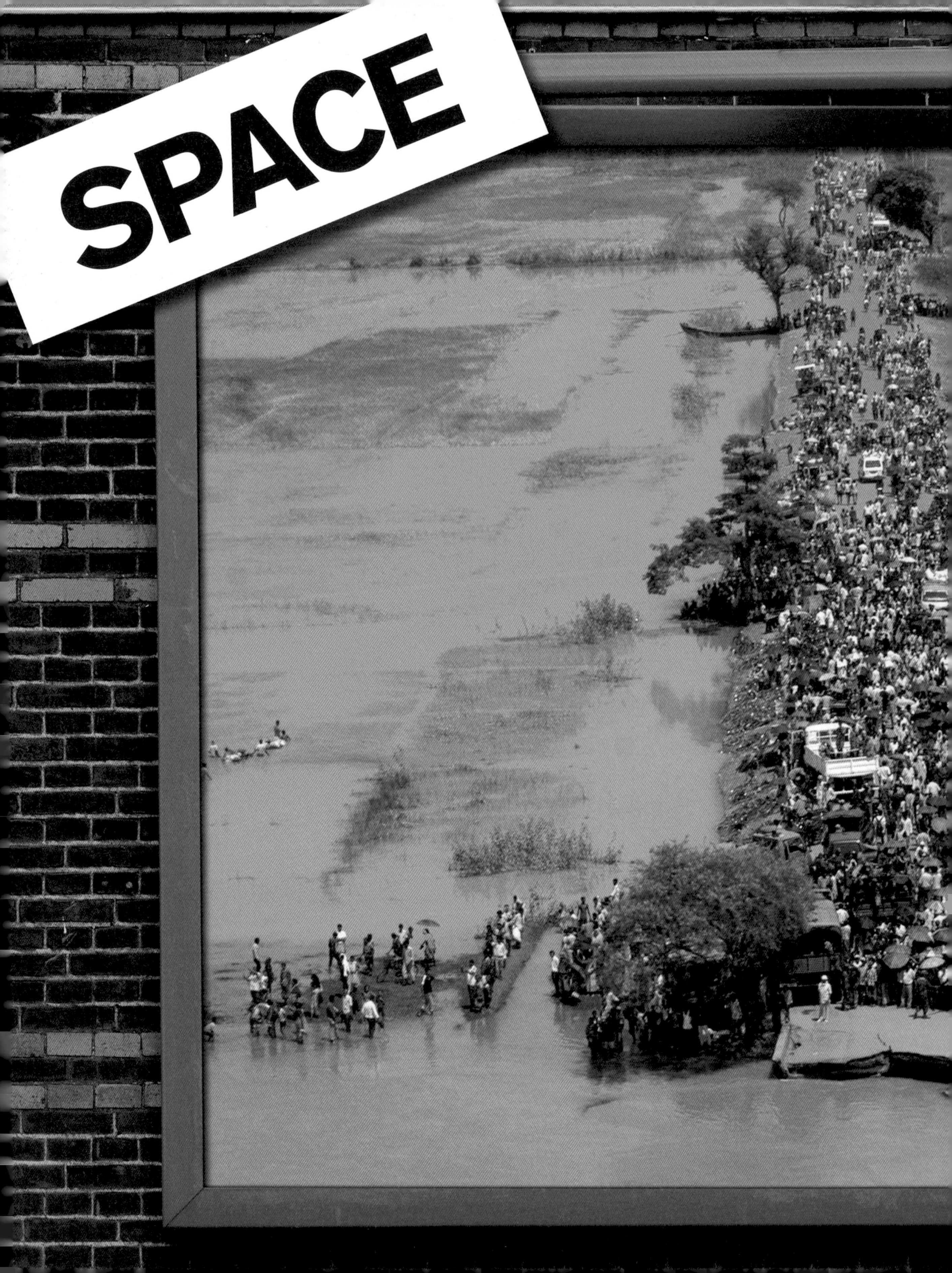
SPACE

Highway in Inarwa
District, 400 kilometres
south-east of Kathmandu,
Nepal, August 2008.

Two-thirds of the world's
population live in endless
urban agglomerations, resulting in
enormous pressure on space. At the
same time valuable space is disappearing as the consequence of a
growing number of natural disasters.

8239

The pressure on space in the Netherlands is concentrated in the Randstad, with the growing claims of housing, agriculture, mobility, recreation and air travel. It is expected that an area the size of the province of South Holland will have to be redesignated to accommodate all these requirements. On the other hand, there is an accelerating process of shrinkage elsewhere in the country.

The search for space for development prior to the design process is becoming untenable. Every millimetre of the city is put to some use, and the combination of functions leads to a polarization of rich and poor.

JCDecaux

3601

JCDecaux

The future lies in the hands of designers able to create space, either by leaving it as it is, or by finding alternatives. There are endless possibilities, such as rezoning assignments, building on water, and multiple use.

2217

EQUAL = UNEQUAL

To counter the uniformity of an area's development, NEXT architects deliberately put their stake on inequality in the form of wide diversity and positive discrimination. By magnifying the intrinsic qualities of each location a multi-faceted living environment is created that has something to offer people of all kinds. This principle can be applied at every scale level, from interior to landscape.

Themes

The *Landscape of labour for the 21st century* will be made up of a great diversity of places of work each with its own quality and parameters. The results of this study are applied in the design for the international advertising agency Wieden + Kennedy. One of their slogans is the famous phrase 'If it feels like work, it isn't working'. The idea that the office is a place for encounter and relaxation as well as a place of work, is perfectly in line with that ideal. The work space is designed as a changeable environment that can accommodate a variety of activities. The types of work on which W+K focuses – network, teamwork and mindwork – are the guiding principle for the design of such work environments.

Landscape of labour for the 21st century is a collaboration between NEXT architects, Erik Wiersema, Joost Mulder, Claudia Linders en Rink Drost.

Photography: Iwan Baan

'While equal rights and equal opportunities are basic values in Western societies, aiming for equality in spatial design all too often results in mediocrity and monotony. The Netherlands is a country where every centimetre of land is at the service of ongoing growth and prosperity and is subject to a desire for control.

A unilateral way of thinking is painfully evident in Dutch government policy on accessibility. The goal of improved accessibility has levelled out the differences between regions and cities. The result is a curious paradox: a country that is too small to begin with tries to become bigger by improving access to the land, but as a result people actually experience a reduction in its size. The contrasts between countryside and city disappear and the countryside degenerates into an urban conglomerate with rural attractions.

As **NEXT** architects see it, the alternative is a country that attempts to hang on to contrasts by adopting inequality as a guiding principle, a country that welcomes diversity and even tries to enhance it. A dynamic urbanism is confronted with a contemporary virgin territory, more difficult to move around in but offering the relief of a slower pace.

This procedure illustrates the ideas of **NEXT**, in which differentiation is regarded as a key concept and every spatial challenge is seen as an appeal to reinforce the identity of a location or condition. To grasp the conditions of a location the firm has developed parameters, underlying values that direct the creation of the right identity in the right design in the right building.

This method can be seen in the study 'Landscape of labour for the 21st century', a visionary study that investigates the spatial consequences of a changing society and with it a changing work environment. The growth and acceleration of communication flows, the ongoing process of individualization, and the goal of even greater wellbeing are changing our everyday reality and how we work. Companies today function as flexible networks in which the individual, the solitary figure who operates in those networks has greater importance. A new Economy of Ideas that assigns a more important role to creativity is emerging, in developments that call for a new work environment.

The **NEXT** study describes that work environment as a creative landscape in which different forms of work dovetail naturally with their surroundings. The primary aim is to enhance the diversity of the work environment. New demands, such as relaxation versus concentration and creativity versus efficiency, are imposed on the quality of the environment in this work landscape. These are the new parameters by which places of work will be judged.' – Bart Reuser, Marijn Schenk and Michel Schreinemachers

1

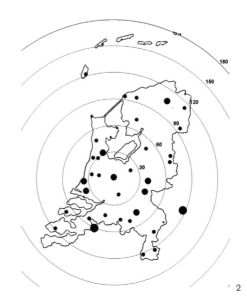

2

The tempographic map indicates distances in minutes of travelling time from the centre rather than in kilometres. The map shows that the Netherlands is equally accessible everywhere, whereas the ideal is a country with far more contrasts.

1 Geographical map NL

2 Tempographic map, car transport

3 Tempographic map, ideal situation

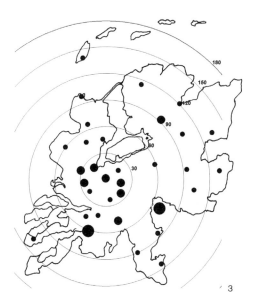

3

Contact
office@oma.com

Office
OMA [Office for Metropolitan Architecture]

ZEEKRACHT

Recognizing that the necessary reorganization of the global energy supply calls for plans that transcend national borders, OMA combines science and architecture on various scales, resulting in a strategy which a sustainable relation between industry and ecology in Europe.

Themes

Legend (top map):
- Int. Ocean Energy Research Station
- Existing Marine Ecological Zone
- Artificial Reef/ Marine Remediation
- Super-Ring Offshore High Voltage
- Onshore High Voltage Power Line
- Superring Energy Export Cable
- Wind Farm
- Wind Turbine Manufacturing/ R&D Center
- Converted Oil/Gas Production
- Shipping Port

North Sea Master Plan
The master plan is a strategic roadmap for renewable energy production in the North Sea, premised upon the maximization of its potential., The master plan proposes the creation of an *Energy Super-Ring* over the coming decades that connects existing and future offshore wind farms to create a constant – and constantly augmentable – source of renewable energy for the surrounding countries and those beyond. The *Production Belt* (blue) mobilizes the industrial resources of the surrounding nations, while the *Reefs* (green) extend and stimulate local marine ecosystems. The *International Research Centre* is envisaged as a shared platform akin to an international space station, centralizing expertise and accelerating the research and development of offshore renewables.

Dutch Sea Master Plan
With its longstanding relationship with the sea, combined with its resources, expertise, industrial potential and geographical location, the Netherlands is poised to take a leading role in driving offshore sustainable energy development. On the national scale, the master plan is designed to meet 2020 targets for renewable energy in a way that stimulates current uses of the Dutch wilderness, i.e. the North Sea. The wind farm developments are multi-purpose clusters of activity, collectively creating a new and dynamic landscape at sea.

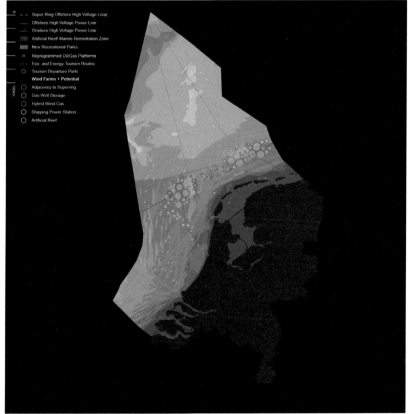

Legend (bottom map):
- Super-Ring Offshore High Voltage Loop
- Offshore High Voltage Power Line
- Onshore High Voltage Power Line
- Artificial Reef/ Marine Remediation Zone
- New Recreational Parks
- Reprogrammed Oil/Gas Platforms
- Eco- and Energy-Tourism Routes
- Tourism Departure Ports
- **Wind Farms + Potential**
- Adjacency to Superring
- Gas Well Storage
- Hybrid Wind-Gas
- Shipping Power Station
- Artificial Reef

Optimized performance
The master plan proposes wind farms arranged in circles, a configuration that clearly defines them as sites and allows symbiotic secondary functions to be embedded in the farms by virtue of their location, extending and promoting marine ecosystems through artificial reef development and tapping industrial resources and systems for mutual productivity.

Dutch Sea Master Plan: micro
Looking in more detail at the circular sites, the individual performance of the turbines and their participatory potential become clear. Particular sites could be affiliated with entities such as cooperatives, cities, companies, and so on. In reaction to perceptions of negative ecological impact, competing claims to areas of the sea, and NIMBYism, the master plan attempts to reposition wind farm development as a positive and productive corollary to the cultural forces currently challenging it.

The integrated system
Circles of wind turbines strung along the *Super-Ring* integrate with gas and oil platforms, shipping routes, and local ecology. In this way, the master plan proposes a new landscape at sea – both figurative and actual – for people to explore and inhabit.

Zeekracht Master plan (2008), Office for Metropolitan Architecture: Rem Koolhaas, Art Zaaijer, Terri Chiao, Talia Dorsey, Christopher Parlato, Franziska Singer, Mark Veldman

'The urgent need for sustainable and secure energy calls for a collective mobilization of intelligence and ambition that transcends standard piecemeal solutions to climate change.

Zeekracht, a master plan for the North Sea, maps out a massive renewable energy infrastructure that engages all the surrounding countries – and potentially those beyond – in a supranational effort that will be both immediately viable and conducive to decades of coordinated development.

The primary components of the Zeekracht master plan include an *Energy Super-Ring* of offshore wind farms – the main infrastructure for energy supply, efficient distribution, and strategic growth; the *Production Belt* – an on-land industrial and institutional infrastructure supporting manufacturing and research; the *Reefs* – integrating ecology and industry by stimulating existing marine life alongside wind turbines and other installations; and an *International Research Centre* – promoting cooperation, innovation and shared scientific development.

Due to its high and consistent wind speeds, shallow waters, and dense surrounding populations with highly developed energy infrastructure and knowledge, the North Sea is arguably the world's best site for large-scale offshore wind farming. The renewable energy that could be harvested from the North Sea annually approaches that currently produced by fossil fuels in the Gulf. With the increasingly desperate need for new sources of energy in the 21st century, the North Sea could – must – become a fulcrum of global energy production.

A master plan for the North Sea cannot be a fixed prescription. The project is conceived as a reciprocal system, fed and reinforced from the top down in technology, industrial development and Europe-wide policy; and from the bottom up in local decision-making, popular involvement and support. For such a multi-layered undertaking on a scale as large as the North Sea, the present is an inappropriate limit. Echoing the ethos of renewable energy, potential must drive development.

Unlike the usual planning methods based on least-conflict zoning, the master plan suggests a multi-dimensional approach based on optimizing potential. The productivity and

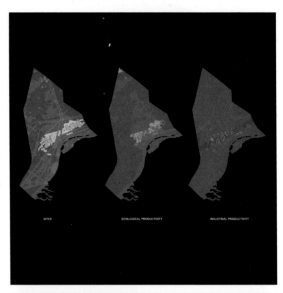

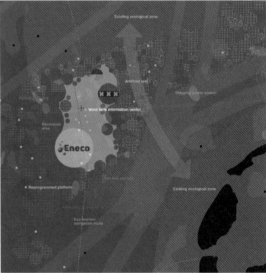

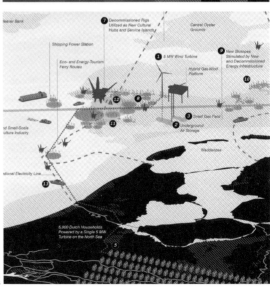

profitability of offshore wind farms can be enhanced if they synergize with existing North Sea activities such as shipping and oil and gas extraction, as well as new programmes such as eco-stimulation and tourism.

The North Sea countries are uniquely positioned to pursue, promote and benefit from research and development in offshore renewable energies – from wind to wave to tidal to biomass. By pooling resources and expertise, the North Sea countries can advance these technologies far beyond today's standards and create a renewable energy infrastructure that places Europe at the forefront of the 21st century's most critical industry.' – OMA

Contact
info@onix.nl

Office
Onix

A NATURING ARCHITECTURE

Designing alternative living environments and applying new techniques that are often handicrafts ensures that the work of Onix looks to the future. Detailed architecture that connects with local history and customs as well as with residents produces an exciting interplay of recognition and astonishment.

Themes

Road bridge in Sneek
The design of the bridge in Sneek combines infrastructure, construction, art and architecture. The contour is reminiscent of the traditional cheese-cover farmhouses in Friesland, while the construction reflects a building expertise that is still present in abundance in the historic town. The boat-like construction of the wooden trusses is a reminder of Sneek as the preeminent water recreation town of the northern Netherlands. All these aspects have led to the first uncovered wooden bridge in the heavy traffic category. This bridge is not just a novelty in the Netherlands but has no precedent in countries like Canada, Norway and Switzerland either, where the covered bridge is a familiar tradition. The bridge is made from Accoya wood, an acetylated timber (modified Radiata Pine, a fast-growing type of tree that is better attuned to the rhythm of life today) which a new factory in Arnhem began processing a year ago. Wood acetylation is a new, sustainable process that renders the wood almost entirely resistant to decay. Wood is a renewable material and thus represents an ecological solution.

Design: OAK (Onix Achterbosch Kunstwerken, a collaboration between Onix and Achterbosch Architectuur)

Photo top: OAK

Photo bottom: Karel Zwaneveld

99

'Architecture begins with an intensive observation of local conditions, traditions, crafts and even folklore. By exposing elements of these to universal and contemporary global influences, fresh combinations of the familiar and the strange are created, a strangely familiar architecture.

We do not look for the static idea of the *genius loci*, but go in search of dynamic environments that elicit constantly changing experiences from the user. In the search for this *scenius loci*, interaction with users is an essential part of the design process, for no project will be viable without them. These buildings and environments are geared to change. They are simple to adapt, so they can move with the times.

To achieve those aims a project is linked in as many ways as possible – conceptually as well as physically – with its surroundings. It forms an *in-between space* that programmes the public and communal space in contrast to the individual space, inviting users to bridge social differences and to share in the use of the space.

These *UNI spaces* acquire significance as zones for social action. The naked, primary architectural image remains open and receptive to such authentic actions as elude preconceived representation. The *undecorated shed* is thus an incomplete architecture that invites a different use; its identity is not fixed but created through the use of the building.

Instead of striving for a perfect conceptual space, we graft our designs onto a living environment. Ideological slickness and capitalist exclusiveness are prevented by an inclusive and hybrid approach to space – a space that is rough and smooth, generic and specific, natural and artificial. This *bush-hammering* of the concept results in a balance between the image and the tactile quality of the building, which is stripped of tectonic autonomy by the rough, informal use of materials.

The random, the exceptional and the unexpected influence the choice of materials through improvisation. This *dirty detailing* brings craftsmanship and industrialization back together and is based as far as possible on renewable, local natural materials that make you want to feel a building with your hands.

This approach to architecture is critical of contemporary culture and of the effects of globalization. Taking one's time, however, is not a principle of slowing down, but a quality-orientated strategy that is opposed to architecture as a commercial consumer article and promotes a personal exclusiveness that is accessible to all. In this non-contemporary attitude we find alternatives for living in the world of the future, which we see reflected in the infinite diversity of architecture, in innovating from project to project and in an intuitive approach to each assignment.

In that future world each project is based on a development of its own. Architecture contributes to the authentic story that people tell about it. The result is a naturing architecture, to which people can relate and which reflects the perfect imperfection of a healthy environment.' – Alex van de Beld and Haiko Meijer

Housing, Egenes Park
Local circumstances, tra-
ditions, crafts – especially
woodworking – and even
folklore are exposed to
today's global influences.
The result is the familiar
yet strange 'shadow
town of Stavanger'.

The buildings are
designed to be adaptable
(some of them form a tem-
porary hotel) and are simple to re-purpose (some
of the houses accom-
modate kindergartens).
The project is related
to the existing wooden
town and the sports park
in scale, material and
expression, reanimating
traditional Norwegian
wooden architecture.
Corridors, transitional and
in-between areas deter-
mine the use by residents,
clients of the kindergarten
and those making use
of the sports facilities,
partly by leaving that use
undefined. The project is
complete and incomplete,
traditional and modern,
urban and rural, repre-
senting an architecture
that is simultaneously
local and universal.
The project was im-
plemented using local
Norwegian wood and
the details are based on
traditional Norwegian
designs and patterns
as they are interpreted
today, using the latest
building techniques.

In cooperation with HLM
Arkitektur AS (NO)

101

EXCLUSIVE PUBLIC SPACE

In addressing dysfunctional public space, Powerhouse Company takes account of the demand by today's society for new forms of social interaction. Its design strategy employs both the opening up and the delimitation of space to find an optimal balance between openness and enclosure to design a public space that meets the requirements of the 21st century.

Themes

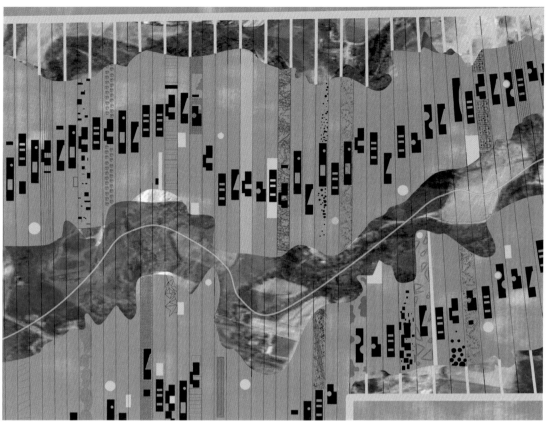

Denmark for All
In recent decades, Denmark has witnessed a phenomenal rise in the number of summer-houses built around the coasts and natural areas. Once primitive retreats, these houses have now become mini-mansions. New developments fail to address the crucial link to the Danish landscape and the new qualities that are emerging. In an attempt to address this situation, Powerhouse Company has analysed the current paradox of Danish summerhouse areas and proposed an alternative model.

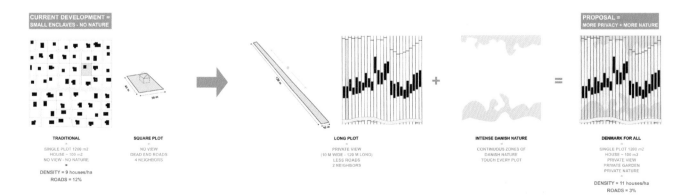

CURRENT DEVELOPMENT = SMALL ENCLAVES - NO NATURE

TRADITIONAL
=
SINGLE PLOT 1200 m2
HOUSE = 100 m2
NO VIEW - NO NATURE
=
DENSITY = 9 houses/ha
ROADS = 12%

SQUARE PLOT
=
NO VIEW
DEAD END ROADS
4 NEIGHBORS

LONG PLOT
=
PRIVATE VIEW
(10 M WIDE - 120 M LONG)
LESS ROADS
2 NEIGHBORS

INTENSE DANISH NATURE
=
CONTINUOUS ZONES OF
DANISH NATURE
TOUCH EVERY PLOT

PROPOSAL = MORE PRIVACY + MORE NATURE

DENMARK FOR ALL
=
SINGLE PLOT 1200 m2
HOUSE = 100 m2
PRIVATE VIEW
PRIVATE GARDEN
PRIVATE NATURE
=
DENSITY = 11 houses/ha
ROADS = 3%

Slinge, XS to XXL

XS: The 30 by 30 centimetres concrete paving stone is the basic element of public space in Rotterdam. It is cheap, modular and indestructible – the basis for vast monotonous surfaces of grey concrete. Around the Slinge metro station, Powerhouse Company proposes a new paving slab, the first one ever to go beyond the paving of neutral space and one which requires a specific behaviour on the part of its user.

S: Young people need places where they can congregate, preferably in prominent public spaces. But what was formerly known as interaction is now often seen as a suspect sort of communality. The *Gangbank* easily accommodates ten to fifteen people and its spatial organization suggests a hierarchical organization. Instead of criminalizing the youngsters who live in this area, the *Gangbank* gives them a prominent place that allows them to immediately become part of the neighbourhood.

M: As an alternative to the dark old bicycle shed beneath the tracks of the Slinge metro station, Powerhouse Company proposes a new bicycle storage facility, designed as a cloud of a thousand lamp posts that fades out into the streets. The plaza in front of the metro station becomes a sea of light that intensifies near the entrance.

'While the classic public space of the historic inner city has been reinstalled as the ideal public space, since the 1980s European historic centres have reclaimed their rights over street life by embracing the dirty equation 'no shopping = no lively public space'. Outside the city centres, in the modernist satellite towns or in the sprawling suburban areas, good communal spaces seem scarce. Either overabundant (as in the modernist satellite towns), or underrepresented (as in the new suburban areas), communal space seems to suffer from its inability to address qualities beyond mere low-maintenance generic greenery.

The need for new forms of communality has been clearly manifested over the last few decades, though in social rather than urban design terms. Whether it is the growing social interest networks on the internet or the rise of small, local entrepreneurs providing local products, new communality revolves around the growing need for specific interests or qualities enjoyed communally.

It is a paradox that we act more and more privately in public space, while private spaces such as shopping centres increasingly use public typologies to create a successful venue. Both tendencies point towards a growing need for specific public space, rather than the generic ideal inherited from the 1960s, as well as a need for less encapsulated private spaces.

Powerhouse Company believes that a careful orchestration of the tensions between public and private spaces can create new types of communal spaces that respond to the paradoxes of everyday reality. For example, public space can be upgraded by making it more personal through the creation of very specific functions While private spaces can be upgraded by adding qualitative public space that gives something back to the landscape instead of just consuming it. In both cases the goal is a productive synergy between the public and the private that is able to transform public space as into platform or fertile ground for progress for the individual as well as the community.

Over the past century there has been a lot of discussion about the merits and demerits of the privatization of public space. This struggle rarely acknowledged the evident dilemma that there is no good use of public space if there is no appropriation. And is appropriation not a form of privatization? This is exactly the problem with most modernist public space – it is hard to appropriate. At the same time the encapsulated sprawling suburban developments are designed to be devoid of any public life or platform for communality. A policy of communalization is needed. Powerhouse Company believes that the new questions of communality cannot be answered without addressing both privatization and publicization in urban design; in other words, without addressing the tension between the individual and the community. Bruno Latour once said: 'If there weren't any walls, it would be impossible to live together in a city.' The question is not just what walls we design, but what doors and windows.'

– Charles Bessard and Nanne de Ru

PRO BLOEMEN   ANTI AUTO&MENSEN

XS

S

L

L: Zuidwijk and Pendrecht are Rotterdam's greenest neighbourhoods, but very few people know that. To improve access to the parks around the Slinge metro station, Powerhouse Company proposes infiltrating the greenery with parking lots instead of situating them around the greenery. This enables people to visit the park without having to leave their car, to have a tailgate barbeque, or to blend the car with the serene green environment. The *Park & Ride* facility connects private transport to public nature.

XL: With the construction of Randstad Rail, a new and faster metro connection due to be completed in 2010, Slinge has enormous potential as a reservoir for parking spaces for visitors to inner-city Rotterdam. Powerhouse Company proposes four *XL Park & Rides*, one for each point of the compass in Rotterdam, clearly branded as entry stations to the city from the motorway. Slinge will become *Park & Ride South*.

XXL: Around Slinge there are 84 hectares of public greenery, but it is standard: mostly grass with boring trees and shrubs. By selling 40 per cent of the public land to the residents, funds are created that can then be invested in the first urban nature development in the Netherlands. Nature organizations and the Dutch Forestry Commission can assist in creating *Slinge Nature City* – a laboratory for the first Dutch urban national park.

XL

M

XXL

TIME

Everything and everybody is permanently online and digitally connected. Seclusion and privacy seem to belong to an archaic era. The timetabling that enabled us to perform different jobs at the same time has been transformed into a temporal order of simultaneity and multitasking.

7544

www.ringelberg.nl

Zoning and functional separation: what began as an efficient planning strategy has become outdated, causing a daily waste of time. Among its results are longer travelling times, especially in the Randstad, where almost 80 per cent of all Dutch traffic jams occur.

Japanese commuters spend the night in cubes because it takes them too long to travel home.

For decades if not centuries architecture was a spatial translation of the average daily routine: separate environments for work, housing, recreation and traffic. Time and place are becoming more and more interchangeable.

A revolution is needed in the physical and mental connection between time and place. Think of architecture that facilitates a clever combination of work and relaxation, think of alternative lifestyles.

7028

JCDecaux

LEF Future Centre in Utrecht, the Netherlands, run by the Netherlands Directorate-General for Public Works and Water Management (Rijkswaterstaat).

Contact
**info@rietveld
landscape.nl**

Office
Rietveld Landscape

A CALL FOR STRATEGIC INTERVEN- TIONS

Given the contemporary complexity of cities, landscape and society, urgent social tasks call for an integral, multidisciplinary approach. Rietveld Landscape's strategic interventions focus and use the forces of existing developments and processes. This design method creates new opportunities for landscape, architecture, the public domain, ecology, recreation and economic activity.

Themes

New Amsterdam Park
is a manifesto for a
new Amsterdam public
domain on the water. It is
prompted by the desire of
residents for a park island
in the harbour, plans for
the construction of a
landing stage for inland
waterways traffic, the
problem of flood tides,
and the protracted debate
about the creation of a
permanent park island
near the KNSM Island.
The floating, temporary
park has three types of
space: water streets and
squares; inner worlds in
large barges; and over-
head routes across the
top of the barges. Some
of the units of the park
are periodically laid out
by and for the use of specific subcultures. Views
between the park units,
overhead routes and a
range of often simple but
effective public meeting
places make it possible to
explore the habits of other
subcultures. The flexibility
of the barges makes the
park highly suitable as a
public domain laboratory.

Design: Rietveld Land-
scape | Atelier de Lyon

Generating Dune Scapes takes advantage of a few gigantic landscape processes in the region where the North Sea Canal flows into the North Sea, as well as already existing urban plans for this region: a sand surplus from the harbour (1.4 million m3 per annum); the plans for the sustainable reuse of residual industrial heat by the Hoogovens steel furnaces (including the establishment of a residual heat company); the redevelopment of the Rivierenbuurt neighbourhood in IJmuiden; and the construction of the biggest lock in the world. These developments create the conditions for one overall intervention and three location-bound strategic interventions. The many empty sites in the area are used for large-scale dune generation, which creates a unique symbiosis between the qualities of the Kennemer Dunes National Park and the urban region. Set against the apocalyptic décor of the Hoogovens furnaces, steaming bunkers and the Kennemer Dunes, the *Hot Spring* will become the first winter spa in Western Europe. The complex of locks will become a landscape of paradoxes as various different kinds of protected bird species find new breeding grounds beside the passing supertankers and cruise ships. The new dune landscape calls for new forms of urban design and architecture, such as the *Sand Wall District*.

'If landscape architecture really wants to make a relevant contribution to the big problems society faces, it is necessary to enter into alliances with researchers, interested parties and specialists. Depending on the assignment, these might be coastal morphologists, historians of architecture or urban geographers. The landscape architect integrates the relevant knowledge at different scale levels and translates this into strategic interventions using a broad set of design skills.

Strategic interventions are precisely chosen and carefully designed urban or landscape interventions that set desired developments in motion. They use the forces of large-scale developments and processes to generate a new context and meaning for qualities that are already present. Apparently contradictory interests and elements on diverse scale levels are linked with one another. The real opportunities for change often lie on a higher scale (such as the regional, national or international level), or in extending the long-term ambitions of the client. Sharp analyses of the possibilities at this strategic level create room for interventions with an important spin-off for society. The meaning, content and quality of our designs is partly based on their relationship with these larger societal issues. The role and experience of various user groups is important in the designs. The interventions stimulate local initiatives or spontaneous use and leave space to be filled in at a later stage. By setting out from subcultures (instead of ethnic backgrounds) with shared interests and concerns, the design brings members of different groups together in a positive and flexible way. This design method leads to unexpected, sometimes paradoxical landscapes and vital public spaces.' – Ronald and Erik Rietveld

Generator

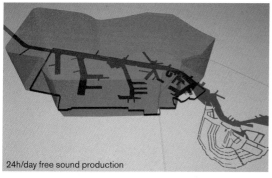

24h/day free sound production

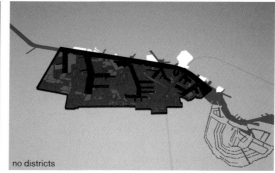

no districts

free heights

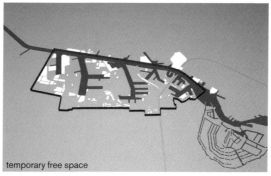

temporary free space

for free spirits

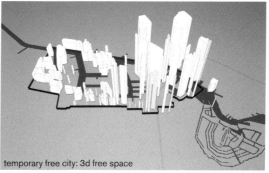

temporary free city: 3d free space

The project *Temporarily Open as Strategy* takes the ambitions of Amsterdam to become one of the best creative cities in Europe seriously. This requires an experimental breeding ground (an underground). To that end, the Amsterdam port authority makes available large-scale temporary locations cheaply and on a temporary basis for initiatives of young talents. They might be disused cargo transit sheds or factory halls, offices, harbour basins, boats or stretches of terrain. Safety and environmental regulations in the port are an obstacle to regular planning, but, ironically, these regulations create unique conditions for a creative free state. For example, people can make as much noise as they like, 24 hours a day, in the port area. Furthermore, in this sea port behind the Westerpark, there are no limitations on construction height. A mysterious fleet of UFOs floats above the port functions as a mobile generator for *The Free Port*. In short, the abundance of rules in this area can be turned to advantage. The port becomes a freezone for experiments by young creative talents.

Design: Rietveld Landscape | Atelier de Lyon

GIVE NATURE MORE SPACE TO SURVIVE

Now and in the future, the countryside deserves to be central to our everyday lives. SeARCH acts to defend our valuable green areas and seeks out alternative space for the countryside and ways to create a greater awareness of the landscape by blurring the boundaries between architecture and nature.

Thema

The *Forest Tower* in Putten is devised as a condensed path with all the attractions of a stroll through the woods, not as a vertical climb. The branches of the tower accommodate various perspectives along the route. Sometimes all you see is the sky, at others you see branches, the ground, or a panorama. Thirty metres above ground level you can clamber over a net to enjoy a performance a little higher up in a small theatre. The end of the walk is not the predictable observatory platform but a new tract of woodland, where you can experiment further with conifers and climb even higher.

Photo: Jeroen Musch

'Each SeARCH project is conceived as a landscape – the most essential and generous element in the design. Without boundaries, landscapes are endless and open; they connect architecture with the urban, interior with exterior. Through the emphasis on landscapes, SeARCH promotes a high degree of sustainability and environmental awareness in its projects. Being Dutch, the designers are well aware of the scarcity of land and strongly believe in using this resource more intelligently in order to give nature more space to survive.

When it comes to ideas, everyday life is a horn of plenty. The strategy of SeARCH is pragmatic. The office assembles information and form to establish a novel relationship between them. The outcome is a collection of highly specific buildings that dovetail with history and function. The context is what already exists, a starting point rather than an authoritative guidebook. SeARCH wants to free architecture from imposed rules and regulations by making it both unpredictable and self-evident.

Architects should focus on creating spaces and cities that are democratic, sensitive, sustainable and tolerant. It sounds simple and obvious, but it isn't. SeARCH questions the merits and banalities of modern civilization that are so obvious in the contemporary city. The office tries to reconnect cultural artefacts with genuinely natural elements.

In order to find you have to **SeARCH**.' – SeARCH

Photography top right
and bottom right:
Jeroen Musch

Contact
stealth@ultd.net

Office
STEALTH.unlimited

CONTEXT DESIGN

STEALTH.unlimited distils the essence of assignments by making thought processes visible in three-dimensional installations. The results of these spatial experiments are analysed with the parties involved to achieve a reformulation of the assignment. It is the assignment itself rather than the final product that is central.

Themes

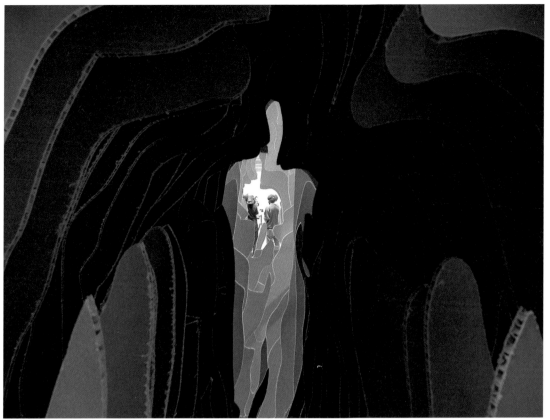

The project *Cut for Purpose* arose from the question of how Museum Boijmans Van Beuningen can use a new museum space to respond to the dynamics of the radically different producers and users of art and culture in Rotterdam. A large group of participants, including curators, artists and the public, investigated which future programmes the museum could develop (for example, an artist in residence programme), which activities it could invite (such as confrontations between representatives of different musical and cultural styles), and how the architectural design of the space could facilitate the chosen activities. While still empty, the future museum space was completely filled with a grid of cardboard panels more than two metres high in which the participants were challenged to cut out the appropriate spatial structure for each situation both on their own and in dialogue with one another. For nine weeks they joined forces to investigate what would be possible in the future space. On the basis of this 1:1 test design, the team of curators decided to abandon any strong programmatic and spatial demands for their programmes and activities because they required a commitment that might well be impossible, given to the present capacities and position of the museum. This dicovery came just in time – before investment in what might have turned out to be an impossible ambition.

'The work of STEALTH.unlimited is focused on questions about space in the city: who produces it, who uses it and how, and what does its future look like? These are important questions given that most societies approach their future prospects increasingly from the standpoint of the individual, while cities are the places in which how we relate to one another now and in the future assumes its most physical and tangible form.

In the last few years STEALTH has been engaged with many participants in intense interdisciplinary projects aimed at formulating, and where possible to finding, answers to these questions. The urban domain is an agency – it is not simply the outcome of architectural and urban design interventions or exclusively the terrain of designers. On the contrary, the urban domain is always an instrument for achieving specific goals, anchoring power positions or outlining futures within the city. It is a force field in which architects, though crucial, have only a limited influence.

Many STEALTH projects and research efforts create a test bed on which the discussion of the future of our built environment is actively encouraged. Various aspects are pinpointed, such as planning versus informality, access to the urban domain, protocols for the use of space, the emancipation of city residents and professionals, and citizen participation in the spatial future of the city.

Working at the interface of architecture and other disciplines creates a much more diverse and innovative workspace, because tools, techniques and concepts emerge that are rarely available, if at all, to architects because of the maddeningly slow development of their profession. At the same time it generates a different sort of result or product than is expected of the average firm of architects. According to STEALTH, one of the key tasks of architects is to design the context in which a specific question or design challenge can be answered. This context does not necessarily – in fact, preferably only by way of exception – lead to a built result.

The built environment is a relatively unsophisticated product that has to meet complex expectations. Right from the start, therefore, one needs to take a sceptical view of its capacity to satisfy all those expectations. Particularly in a social context and an economic situation in which the emphasis is increasingly on the content, the software, rather than the built hardware, architecture has to embrace a new professional and social commitment.' – Ana Dzokic and Marc Neelen

Contact
**studio@marco
vermeulen.nl**

Office
Studio Marco Vermeulen

SUPER-NATURAL

The underlying concept in the work of Studio Marco Vermeulen is the reciprocity between programme, location and raw materials. **New programmatic alliances and typologies** emerge by linking these in an intelligent way, contributing to the broadening of the discipline of architecture.

Themes

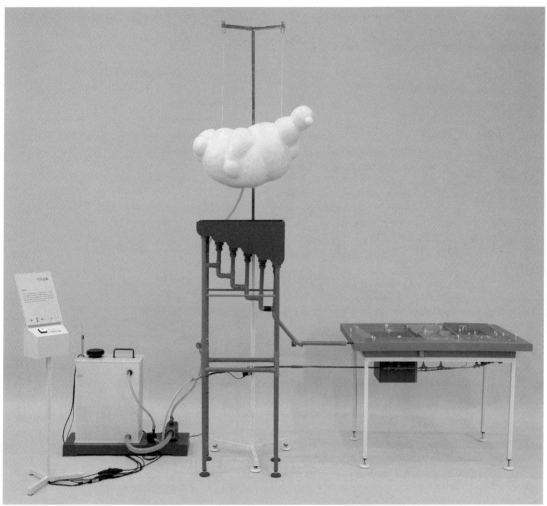

Water squares, Rotterdam
It will rain more heavily and more often in the near future. Instead of increasing the capacity of subterranean drainage, flood squares are implemented in Rotterdam to integrate water retention into an attractive public area. A flood square changes its appearance and use after a heavy shower.

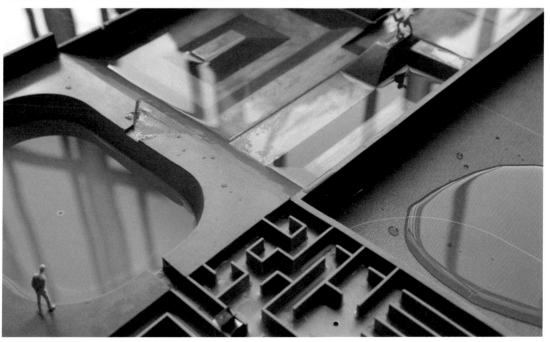

'The ever-increasing worldwide demand for energy, food and raw materials obliges us to consider fundamentally new directions and strategies while preserving and restoring eco-systems. Many current issues of varying scales are drawn together in the spatial design that will be needed to explore, inspire and guide the process of designing the brief. Integration with other fields of knowledge is essential. Architecture will have to become a catalyst of social renewal and a stimulus to technological innovation, a challenge beyond the mere addition of new technologies to existing spatial typologies. Many of the new challenges call for typological innovation, a fundamental reorientation of the existing spatial models and connections that calls for a healthy dose of positivism and originality.

A good design addresses several issues at the same time and creates value for as many aspects as possible. Studio Marco Vermeulen sees a key to economic, ecological and social profitability in the elimination of contradictions in the brief and the maximized combination of functions. For instance, the asphalted public area in the city can be designed in such a way that it also functions as a buffer for precipitation during heavy downpours. This entails a new typology – the water retention square – an attractive public place that encourages social contact and exchange while at the same time contributing to sustainable urban water management.
The spatial design for Clover 4 Greenport Venlo demonstrates an original design approach to industrial estates, which are often seen as a violation of the landscape and the environment in which we live, even though many people spend a large part of their lives in them.

The strategic positioning and conscious design of a number of water management facilities results in an attractive work environment in a functional landscape.
A major ecological and economic advantage can be gained by combining functions that require a lot of energy, water and raw materials at the same location. Clustering and, where possible, stacking these functions enables the mutual exchange of surpluses and residual products, so that a large number of cycles can be self-contained on location.

While many technological developments have made us more distant from the world, architecture is able to give form to the renewed alliance with the elements and ecosystems, accommodating such an alliance by making it visible and legible, contributing to the awareness of interdependence. It is a great challenge to work with technological advances and scientific insights on new spatial solutions and typologies that facilitate a healthy and attractive residential environment. A vital architecture forms a synthesis between buildings and landscape in a natural and original way and expresses the interaction with the surroundings and the elements.' – Marco Vermeulen

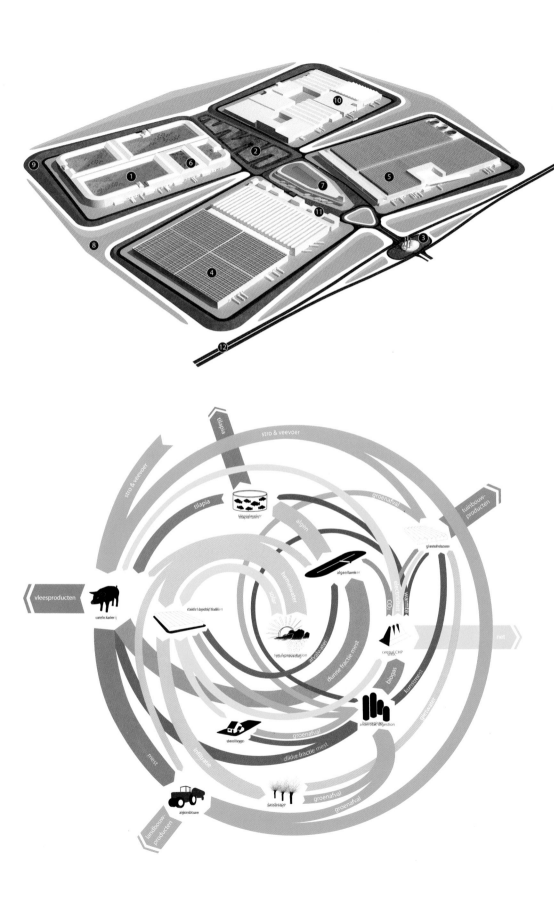

Clover 4 Greenport Venlo
A large-scale work land-
scape is being developed
to the north-west of Venlo
in which logistics, agri-
culture and greenhouse
cultivation can draw the
maximum benefit from
each other's presence.
The four-leafed clover
structure of the spatial
hub of the masterplan
facilitates the exchange
of energy, water and
residues between the
different enterprises, as
well as with the surrounding natural landscape
that penetrates deep into
the clover leaf itself.

1   stacked livestock
    farming and logistics
2   biological water
    purification/algae farm
3   thermal energy plant/
    bio fermentation plant
4   sun field
5   stacked green-
    house cultivation
    and logistics
6   tilapia farm
7   collective amenities
8   water retention
    and infiltration
9   basis
10 agribusiness
11 offices
12 Greenport lane

Designs: Studio Marco
Vermeulen / Urban Af-
fairs in cooperation with
De Urbanisten / VHP

SOCIAL COHESION

Digitization, migration, secularization and the atomization of the use of time seem to have reduced social cohesion. Gated communities are appearing even outside conflict zones. The use of CCTV monitoring is on the increase in public spaces. A society in which people turn their backs on one another looms.

In the last few years the Netherlands has been faced with growing socio-psychological polarization. Besides the uniform Vinex housing estates, which offer hardly any insight into the diversity of society, forty problem neighbourhoods have been identified in which disagreements often erupt into conflict. There are few national symbols or commemorations that everyone can identify with.

7022

JCDecaux

A culture of fear and recrimination has its own architecture of avoidance and blockade.

Design can contribute to a social climate in which other people can be rediscovered or seen in a new light. This must be organized not just by government; the responsibility lies with the population as well.

Contact
**info@urban
unlimited.nl**

Office
Urban Unlimited

ARTICULA-TION IN THE NETWORK SOCIETY

Urban Unlimited is characterized by a pro-active approach towards today's network society. By linking enterprising actors and various disciplines at regional level unique alliances are formed that use local specifics to optimal effect.

Themes

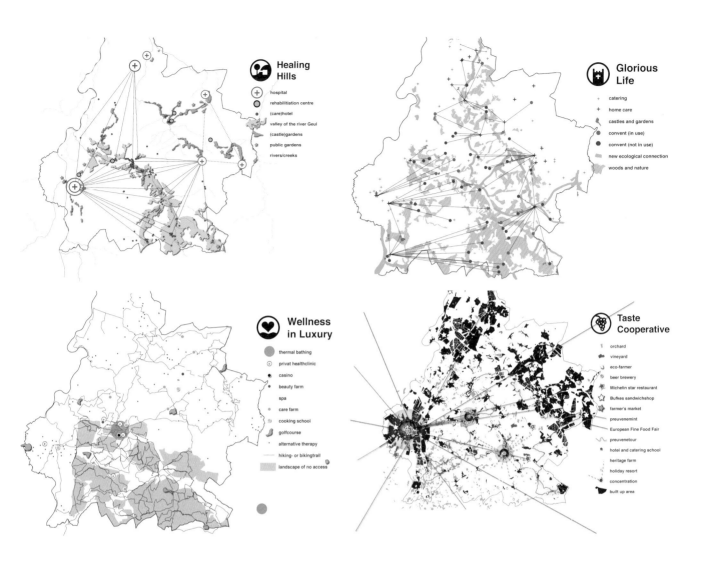

Healing Hills

⊕ hospital
◉ rehabilitiation centre
• (care)hotel
  valley of the river Geul
  (castle)gardens
  public gardens
  rivers/creeks

Glorious Life

+ catering
+ home care
  castles and gardens
● convent (in use)
● convent (not in use)
  new ecological connection
  woods and nature

Wellness in Luxury

● thermal bathing
⊕ privat healthclinic
• casino
• beauty farm
  spa
• care farm
  cooking school
  golfcourse
• alternative therapy
— hiking- or bikingtrail
  landscape of no access

●

Taste Cooperative

  orchard
  vineyard
  eco-farmer
  beer brewery
  Michelin star restaurant
☆ Bufkes sandwichshop
  farmer's market
  preuvenemint
  European Fine Food Fair
  preuvenetour
• hotel and catering school
  heritage farm
  holiday resort
  concentration
  built up area

139

'Over the past decade or two Urban Unlimited has observed that the inflation of plans is a phenomenon that causes little concern. The value and significance of the visionary spatial plan have been reduced to virtually zero, while architects still delight in drawing them. Overproduction is due to designs no longer being subjected to the discipline of committed principals, solid argumentation or a realistic implementation trajectory. Design has in fact become an autonomous cultural product, whose authorship is more important than the building itself.

Ever since its foundation in 2000 Urban Unlimited has focused on the forces behind the network society that are responsible for the plural meanings sites take on and for changes over time. The firm is constantly aware of this and aims at adjusting the existing physical space to reflect new connections and changing demands that reinforce specific local qualities. Physical entities are not neutral platforms or containers where everything that is in fashion at the moment can take place; they have a specific function in time, place and networks.

Space is a dynamic entity that is continually constructed by many processes and actors in shifting networks and alliances. Urban Unlimited tries to reformulate each assignment accordingly. For instance, it is less interested in whether and how an expansion of Schiphol Airport can be organized, than in how the airport system can distinguish itself in the global network and be better linked to the regional economy and its socio-cultural context. Interventions that take account of such links will benefit both Schiphol and the region.

Urban Unlimited is fundamentally focused on cross-overs and actors, rather than the literal translation into spatial plans or buildings. It targets the interaction between agents and disciplines that until recently, or even today, rarely come into contact with one another, such as housing and health care, the economy and nature, leisure and religion, design and jurisprudence, and government and enterprises. Cross-overs are fundamental in the search for highly specific local network opportunities.

Urban Unlimited analyses a brief thoroughly to determine what extra-governmental participation it requires; heterogeneous forces can be found in persons and objects connected with a particular issue or theme. The actors are tempted into new alliances and solutions that add extra value to the predicted results and can be used to reconstruct the site and region in a new and more sustainable way. In contrast to common practice in spatial design, the firm is more interested in the people, enterprises and stories of the location and the network than in a plot of land that requires a layered approach to development.

A typical physical intervention concerns the renovation of old family hotels to make them suitable for wheelchairs. This was one of the links in an entirely new care network in which a hospital could cooperate with hotels and leisure entrepreneurs, enabling patients to recover more quickly and effectively from surgery. This produces results at several levels: the analyses lead to awareness of the as yet unknown qualities of an often already familiar region, the alliances lead to business cases in which a location is put on the global map in a new relational way and the images are interactively built up to form a vision with which the relevant entrepreneurs, residents and administrators concerned can identify, both financially and politically.' – Luuk Boelens and Wies Sanders

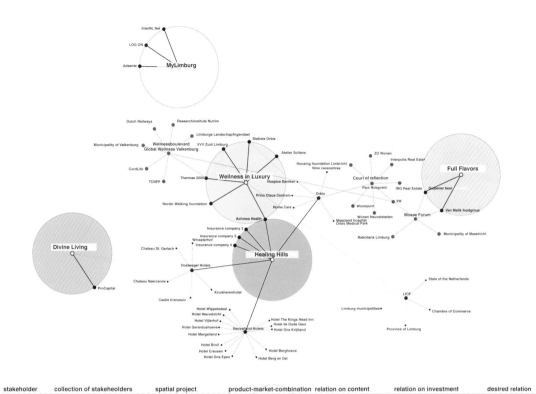

stakeholder collection of stakeholders spatial project product-market-combination relation on content relation on investment desired relation

Heerlijkheid Heuvelland
The dwindling tourist industry around Valkenburg motivated a search for appropriate new markets for a precious landscape, taking into account small-scale entrepreneurs. The core qualities of the region were analysed and linked to new, powerful markets such as health care, real estate (still a strong market in 2005) and retail. This produced four opportunities in which the new markets would support the existing qualities of the landscape and strengthen their business operations. The best-known of these opportunities is *Healing Hills*, in which the Orbis hotel and Heuvelland Hotels provide convalescent holidays in the Heuvelland area. The patients recover better and more quickly, the hospital saves money, and the hotels have managed to fill the dips in the season.

141

Contact
**post@vanberg
enkolpa.nl**

Office
Van Bergen Kolpa Architecten

AN ARCHITEC-TURE OF GROWTH

The space around us is in a constan state of flux. Van Bergen Kolpa Architecten designs architecture that can adapt to such dynamism at every scale level by seeking a balance between programme, landscape and natural resources. The architecture derives its raison d'être from contemporary and future processes.

Themes

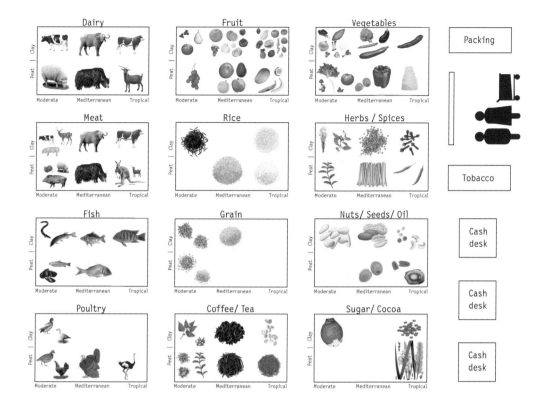

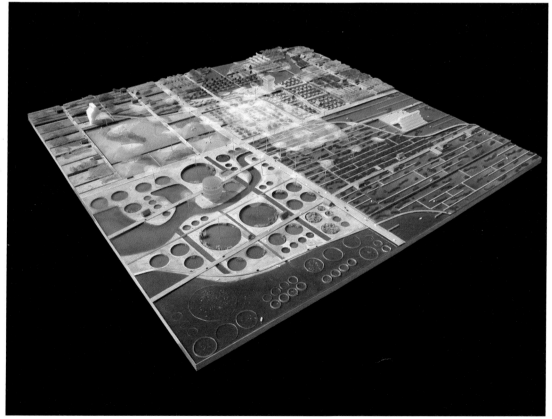

Park Supermarket is a spatial developmental model for a national supermarket located in the metropolitan parks of the Randstad. The polder landscape of Holland, once the public image of our food-producing landscapes, has now been subsumed within expanding city boundaries and has become wetter under the pressure of climate change and the bedding down of the soil but it still needs to meet the demand for food production and recreation for the widely varied population of the Randstad with its many different cuisines.

A completely new landscape will be created in easily accessible locations such as Midden Delfland, chosen for their soil types (peat and clay), a higher water level and new climatic zones (temperate, Mediterranean and tropical) for the growing of products commonly sold in a modern supermarket. Each department will have its characteristic range and product type, such as pandan and risotto rice grown on stepped terraces, tilapia fish in meandering pools, and kiwis and avocados grown against undulating fruit walls. The climate control of the supermarket in the open air would be provided by traditional techniques such as heat-accumulating serpentine walls combined with contemporary solutions such as an insulating mist roof and heating that makes use of the warmth of ground-source heat pump.

Through its fine-meshed structure in one-hectare plots, *Park Supermarket* can grow to keep pace with the diversity in consumer food demand and new agricultural techniques to enable consumption and recreation in a new Randstad park landscape tailored to the 21st century.

Park Supermarket is commissioned by Stroom Den Haag and the province of Zuid-Holland (South- Holland).

143

'Architecture visualizes and defines the future. Its force of imagination is provocative and a generator of new concepts for development. Its material form pins down, defines and makes tangible the future. Right now, when fundamental questions about our future food and energy supply, social relations, natural resources and the environment we live in are raised daily, it is the architect's task to come up with spatial design solutions. Such design is not limited to a building, or a city, but extends from the molecular scale of water and oxygen to the heat-accumulating mass of cities and to a growing landscape. It is a spatial constellation that orchestrates materials, people and energy into a cohesive whole, a spatial model of an architecture of growth.

Just as architecture can define and sum up, architectural design can analyse the brief. Van Bergen Kolpa Architecten organizes this process around a balance of three main elements: programme (economy), landscape (space), and natural resources (social relevance). The economic basis laid down by the principal is placed in the context of the characteristics of the location and their social relevance. Our designs function as a dynamic system or ecology that creates the spatial conditions for economic and social developments.

The design practice of Van Bergen Kolpa Architecten focuses on architecture as a project of transformation over growth time that defines the ambition and innovative potential of the project for the future. In our view, the task of architecture is to programme projects with a condensed growth time, such as a specific construction project, in such a way that they can offer long-term prospects for development or transformation. Conversely, the vision development and research of long growth times such as those of a city or landscape have to be linked to a conceivable opportunity in the near future. Such an approach will create new architectural typologies that offer solutions for our food and energy supply, social relations, natural values and our environment.' – Jago van Bergen and Evert Kolpa

STORMVOGEL Nabuurschap Hoogvliet Vestia – Estrade Projecten van Bergen Kolpa Architecten		BORDER GARDEN				FLORAL GARDEN			FRUIT GARDEN		
A	North-east sun, hedge adjacent to building, bordering on public area.	lonicera japonica halliana		hedera colchica "dentata variegata"	hydrangea petiolaris	rosa "parkdirektor riggers"		hydrangea petiolaris	hedera colchica "dentata variegata"		
B	North-east sun, hedge adjacent to building, bordering on private area.	vitis coignetiae	wisteria sinensis "prolific"		clematis tangutica	rosa "pink cloud"	vitis coignetiae	wisteria sinensis "prolific"			
C	North-west and north-east sun, freestanding hedge, bordering on public area.	aristolochia durior	vitis coignetiae	parthenocissus tricolor "veitchii boskoop"	clematis montana "mayleen"	campsis tagliabuana "madano galen"	lonicera jap "dart's acumen"	leipeer – lelappel			
D	North-west sun, hedge adjacent to building, bordering on garden or public area.	akebia quinata	wisteria flor "honbeni"	hedera colchica "sulphur heart"	clematis montana "freda"	wisteria floribunda "shiro noda"		hydrangea petiolaris	leipeer – lelappel	vitis boskoops glory	
E	Sun from all sides, freestanding hedge, bordering on communal area.	lonicera jap "dart's acumen"	euonymus fortunei "coloratus"	parthenocissus tricolor "veitchii boskoop"	clematis "hagley hybrid"	clematis "jackmanii superba"		rubus tricolor	chaenomeles superba "fusion"		
F	South-west and south-west sun, freestanding hedge, bordering on public area.	clematis montana "freda"	clematis armandii	clematis tangutica	rosa "compassion"	ceanothus "gloire de versailles"	jasminum nudiflorum	rubus phoeniculatus	rosa canina	rosa pendulina	
G	South-west or south-east sun, hedge adjacent to building, bordering on garden or public area.	wisteria sinensis "prolific"	hydrangea petiolaris	clematis orientalis "orange peel"	campsis radicans "flava"	campsis tagliabuana "madame galen"	rosa "zephirine drouhin"	vitis book. glory	vitis "vroege v.d. laan" schisandra chinensis "eastern prince"		
H	South-west and south-east sun, freestanding hedge, bordering on public area.	euonymus fortunei "variegatus"	euonymus fortunei "coloratus"	hedera helix	jasminum nudiflorum	clematis montana "freda"		rubus"spect.tayb." rubus "autumn bliss" rubus "thornil.loganb." rubus "thornless evergreen"			

144

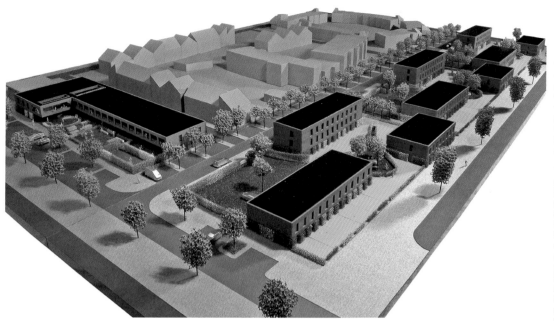

The *Nabuurschap* design is intended to create a new, small-scale urban module for the garden town of Hoogvliet. Contemporary social relations take root only with difficulty in the original structure of such new towns as Hoogvliet, with their expanse of public greenery. Can communities breathe new life into this town on the basis of communal amenities?

The design defines a new balance between housing, social relations and greenery. Clusters of ten or so family homes with gardens would be built around communal courtyards that serve as spaces for children to play, or to hold a community summer party, or for a game of jeu de boules. Collective resources such as rainwater and waste are collected in the communal garden and used to irrigate and fertilize the green oasis. The forecourt to each *Nabuurschap* cluster offers parking space for cars and bikes.

In each *Nabuurschap* cluster communal activities could expand over time, depending on how the residents choose to use the space, but each cluster would grow into a green wall of blossom and fruit trees, offering a constantly changing view to the residents through the seasons. A new growing New Town for the 21st century.

Nabuurschap is commissioned by Estrade Projecten, Rotterdam.

Photo: Jeroen Musch

LIVING TO-GETHER IN THE ERA OF GLOBAL-IZATION

VenhoevenCS aims to enable autarkic urban life in which the question of sustainability is closely linked with the demands of the multicultural society. Existing social structures are served by a low-consumption, productive living environment.

Themes

Sportplaza Mercator is a new initiative for the multicultural Baarsjes district of Amsterdam. The building is designed as a miniature society, a city in a building, in which the whole community is served. The interior looks like an urban network with alleyways, framed views and many different functions, such as an indoor swimming pool with therapy baths, a fitness centre, a room for parties, a café-restaurant, and a Kentucky Fried Chicken outlet. Because the visitors can see one another and the different activities, they are introduced to other cultures and activities. The outside of the building is covered entirely with vegetation so that it becomes an extension of the adjacent Rembrandt Park.

Photography:
Luuk Kramer

'To deal more efficiently with the available space and sources of energy, architects will have to shed immutable design traditions in a search for new solutions. Low-energy buildings and sustainable materials are essential if we are to find a solution to today's environmental problems, but more is needed for a genuinely self-sufficient urban life. Cities and public spaces must be made attractive, productive and prosperous meeting places again by combining designers' cultural, technical and organizational innovations.

Traffic movements could be made redundant to eliminate the noise and pollution they cause. A reduced volume of traffic and more sustainable mechanized transport would slash CO_2 emissions and contribute to world health. We can achieve a reduction in the volume of mechanized transport by combining all the functions of city life and by making cities produce food and energy.

Various successful alternatives can be found in world history for housing, mobility and encounter. Examples include the medieval cities with their short walking distances and local food production, Roman baths, the intelligent infrastructure of some cosmopolitan cities and the compact, mixed structure of favelas. But the sustainable urban environments of tomorrow are no longer the homogeneous cities of the past. They have become much more cosmopolitan. The increase in international communication, trade, tourism and migration means we must learn to deal with cultural diversity.

Traditions, norms and values can no longer be taken for granted when different population groups come together. Sustainable cities will therefore have a different look about them. VenhoevenCS designs cities, public buildings and public spaces in which the multicultural society is blended to form a smoothly functioning whole. To that end we design public buildings as cosmopolitan miniature cities clad in a skin. Society can be rejuvenated here by encounters with people who would otherwise live completely separate lives. The external appearance of these buildings can be interpreted in a variety of ways, while in the complex interior the view of other spaces, cultures and users is the prime focus.

In spatial and cultural terms, the sustainable designed cities and buildings of VenhoevenCS are a patchwork of different cultures, a lively cosmopolitan whole and an ideal biotope for pedestrians. By combining all urban functions including food and energy production, health care and waste processing in high-density locations, regions can become self-sufficient and new areas of natural beauty can be created close to the cities.' – Ton Venhoeven

*City of Cities,
South Korea*
In City of Cities, a
proposal for the new city
of Chungcheongnam in
South Korea, village, town
and metropolitan environ-
ments are concentrated
in an area that covers
only 18 of the available
73 square kilometres.
Nature predominates in
the surrounding districts.
The development of the
urban design is aimed at
discovering how cities can
be made completely self-
sufficient and emission-
free in the long term. The
urban fabric is composed
of various urban islands,
each of which is a part of
the metropolis but at the
same time a fully fledged,
car-free village or town
with mixed functions. To
prevent unplanned urban
sprawl growth is only al-
lowed within the city limits.

VenhoevenCS in coop-
eration with Ton Schaap
(Dienst Ruimtelijke
Ordening Amsterdam),
Herman Zonderland
(Dienst Ruimtelijke Orden-
ing Amsterdam), René
Kuiken, Cees van Giessen

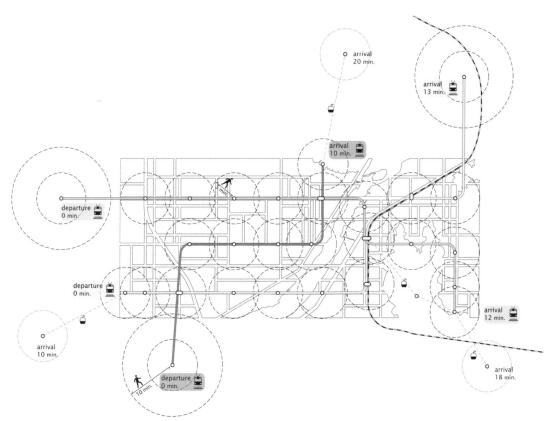

HAPPY ISLANDS

Embroidering on the Dutch tradition of creating land, West 8 has developed a strategy for underrated areas, starting with the Randstad. New land offers plenty of opportunities to break radically with old customs and habits in environmental planning. Design can be fully attuned to the demands of the future.

Themes

The *Happy Islands* plan is a Dutch-Flemish collaboration by West 8 urban design & landscape architecture and Svasek Hydraulics, Coastal, Harbour & River Engineering Consultants.

1 Plan of *Happy Islands*, January 2008, between 5 and 25 kilometres from the coast. The rising sea level can be absorbed for the next 100 years. The first island to be created, opposite the estuary of the Westerschelde, would reduce the floodtide water level by half a metre.

Den Helder

IJmuiden

Amsterdam

Zandvoort

Den Haag

Hoek van Holland   Rotterdam

Vlissingen

Zeebrugge

Oostende

Duinkerken

'The delta of the Lowlands is one of the most densely populated regions in the world. Unlike the districts around London or Paris, for example, a unique metropolis has developed here with an indefinable appearance. The Randstad and the Flemish Diamond are agglomerations without beginning or end, an amalgamation of suburbs and suburban villages, industrial estates, retail parks, harbours and infrastructure interspersed with fragments of authentic agrarian landscape. This peripheral landscape is losing its attractiveness and its prospects. The Delta metropolis is becoming less and less popular because of the steady disappearance of the open countryside and because of the rising sea level that directly threatens low-lying land. Who will want to live on this land without a horizon or farmers at the plough? What are the prospects for a cluttered metropolis given anti-urban sentiment and an anonymous residential environment.

The obvious solution is to offer the Randstad and the Flemish Diamond new prospects – new land in the form of a series of artificial islands off the coast of Flanders, Zeeland and Holland. These dune islands, with a total surface area of more than 150,000 hectares, will break the waves that are rising in front of the vulnerable coast. Engineering the channels will improve the offshore undercurrent so that the sea level drops when a storm blows from the northwest.

The main island, *Hollandsoog*, 150,000-200,000 hectares, will be shaped like Terschelling, a happy island for families, lonely hearts, poets and festivals. Hollandsoog could develop an economy based on leisure activities and the enjoyment of nature. City folk short of space and relaxation could have an inexpensive home in the country. A dacha for every family! Reliable ferry services will take people from the cities to the seaside in the weekends and school holidays. Protected from the worst of the sea, the old mainland will remain the place for daily traffic, school and work.

A new delta will be developed off the coast of Zeeland with smaller islands, tidal channels and salt marshes. The northernmost island of this offshore delta will be Nieuw Voorne, a place for isolated nature, high-risk industry and harbour functions as well as energy such as a nuclear power station and a liquid gas terminal. The southernmost island of the offshore delta, the new, flat and elongated surface of Ra, will be protected by a narrow strip of dunes. The central island, opposite the Oosterschelde, is intended as an island for nature and a waterfront town.

An island will be created off the coast of Flanders with a surface area twice the size of Brussels-Halle-Vilvoorde as much-needed new land for nature and the expansion of the harbour of Antwerp outside the dike, with considerable significance for the community.

The *Happy Islands* will house a continuous windmill park to make the islands self-sufficient in energy as well as generating twenty per cent of the energy requirements of the mainland. The creation of deep troughs for sand excavation will mean the restoration of a resting and breeding ground for fish in this special habitat. A larger diversity of species will be able to develop, to the benefit of the fishery sector.

By combining and harmonizing a variety of interests the islands will be a sustainable gift to future generations. The Happy Islands are a fascinating addition to the rich Dutch tradition of making land.' – Adriaan Geuze

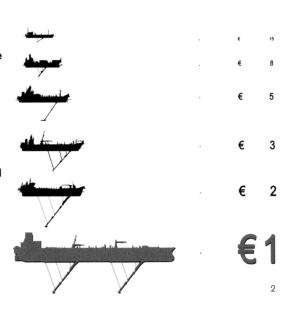

€ 15

€ 8

€ 5

€ 3

€ 2

€ 1

2

2 Making use of larger vessels and other in-novative solutions leads to greater efficiency, reduces costs and opens new perspectives.

3 Cross-section of the trough from which the sand is excavated. The troughs will form a special habitat with new resting and breeding grounds for several species of fish.

4 The technology for creating land above sea level is not new. The Netherlands already has more than 23,000 hectares of landfill.

3

■ Landfill and impoldering

■ ~22.500 Ha in total

4

Contact
info@zus.cc

Office
ZUS [Zones Urbaines Sensibles]

RE-PUBLIC

Architecture has become marginalized in the last two decades by responding mainly to the demands of the market. ZUS puts the public role of the architect back at the centre by making social challenges explicit with <mark>unsolicited architecture and architectural activism</mark>.

Themes

Neo-localism: uninvited architecture for the city
Neo-localism is a reaction to the quasi-urban design that has been implemented in the last twenty years on neo-liberal principles. Neo-localism is based on the notion that, in spite of the inevitable global migration and flows of capital, sustainable urban districts can only thrive if they have local roots. This means respect for the existing physical and social structures. In the Rotterdam city centre ZUS calls for a ban on demolition to link the necessary densification with the street. The plinth accommodates a *local trade centre* as a riposte to the *global trade centre*. Such opposition gives the location its character.

'Architecture has always had an explicitly public aspect, particularly in the cities, and in the last couple of decades attention has swung to the expressiveness of spectacular buildings.

But a city is more than the decor of a collection of buildings; it is the public structures in and around which private parties make their dreams come true. Particularly in the European city, and increasingly in the United States and Asia, the public domain is the crystallization of democracy, the setting for social confrontation and encounter.

The neo-liberal forces of the last twenty years have fragmented the physical appearance of the city into an archipelago lacking direction or alignment, kept alive solely by processes of participation. The public domain is being eroded by far-reaching privatization and the retreat of government that places pressure on its public nature and its democratic significance.

Re-public stands for the enrichment of the urban public structures by a combination of long-term vision and spontaneous informal development. Re-public emphasises the notion of a clear separation between public and private responsibilities in urban production. Public bodies can develop sustainable structures, while private forces can work in a very site-specific and sensitive way.

Architects and urban designers need to be socially challenged to ensure that public values such as cultural historical, socio-economic diversity and the public domain are guaranteed. If this is not already obvious within the framework of the assignment, uninvited architecture and architectural activism are methods of making this agenda visible. Plans for the future can point out where the problems in the present situation lie, but should not remain confined to analysis. It is the putting forward of proposals that renders visible the potential of a location and that can mobilise the public debate. By deploying architectural resources on a small scale to demonstrate how things can be done differently and better, perhaps architecture will be taken seriously again in the social debate.'
– Elma van Boxel and Kristian Koreman

**Universal Rights of Man **
chapter of minimal public space per citizen

Supported by Unesco, a new branch has been formed to protect a critical amount of public space in each city. Based on a quota of their density and available public space each city has been protected against further privatization and increasing repression.
As an extension of the Universal Rights of Man a chapter of minimal public space per citizen was added to be able to supervise the global threat of privatization.

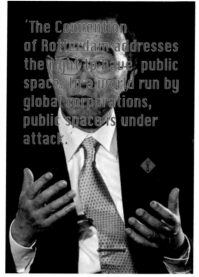

'The Convention of Rotterdam addresses the right to have public space. In a world run by global corporations, public space is under attack.'

European Institute for sufficient publicness

It is meant to judge over any kind of privatization development in order to prevent monopoly of public space possession and control by a single corporation.

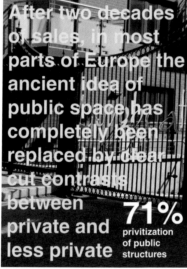

After two decades of sales, in most parts of Europe the ancient idea of public space has completely been replaced by clear-cut contrasts between private and less private **71%** privitization of public structures

protecting against
PUBLIC DEVELOPMENT BOARD ROTTERDAM

liquidations in the cultural circuit, which disregards historical values, local economies and urban structures in order to strive for true diversity

ROTTERDAM GLOCAL DISTRICT

Public Domain Campaign
While there are plenty of frameworks, regulations and institutes for the environment, food and economic activities there is not a single guarantee for the extremely vulnerable public domain. Creeping privatization of the public domain is a direct attack on the democratic system that has been carefully built up and cherished over centuries. This campaign calls for a constant monitoring and guarantee of minimal values.

157

Evicted families find a new place to stay outside the city, Sacramento, California, United States, March 2009.

€ **The financial crisis is penetrating every layer of society. The state of the economy has become a public issue par excellence. It is becoming clear that the privatization of profits and socialization of losses has become excessive.**

Hillenaar

If the Netherlands continues on its present course, there will soon be no more purely Dutch business activities. Even the providers of utilities that offer public services are passing into the hands of global players. The crisis is hitting the building industry hard despite desperate attempts by government to stimulate building.

€ Retail value and price of production are not the same as social value. In the last few years the economic value of architecture has only too often been reduced to its real estate value. Little quality building takes place because of a limited conception of costs.

Happiness

HUTAN

€ Broadening the notion of value
to the longer term and the social
context creates new space, both
mentally and physically: physically in
the form of architecture that does not
separate functions but links them;
mentally in the form of changes of
perspective.

CREDITS

This publication coincides with the international travelling exhibition 'Architecture of Consequence', by the Netherlands Architecture Institute.

Editorial team: **Ole Bouman (editor in chief), Anneke Abhelakh, Mieke Dings, Ingrid Oosterheerd, Martine Zoeteman (managing editor)**
Translation: **Peter Mason**
Copy editing: **Rowan Hewison**
Design: **De Designpolitie**
Photography billboards: **Gerrit Serné**
Printing: **Die Keure**
Production: **Caroline Gautier (NAi Publishers), Martine Zoeteman (NAI)**
Publisher: **Eelco van Welie (NAi Publishers)**

NAi Publishers is an internationally orientated publisher specialized in developing, producing and distributing books on architecture, visual arts and related disciplines.
www.naipublishers.nl

Available in North, South and Central America through D.A.P./Distributed Art Publishers Inc, 155 Sixth Avenue 2nd Floor, New York, NY 10013-1507, tel +1 212 627 1999, fax +1 212 627 9484, dap@dapinc.com

Available in the United Kingdom and Ireland through Art Data, 12 Bell Industrial Estate, 50 Cunnington Street, London W4 5HB, tel +44 208 747 1061, fax +44 208 742 2319, orders@artdata.co.uk

Printed and bound in Belgium

ISBN 978-90-5662-726-3

ILLUSTRATION CREDITS

ACKNOWLEDGEMENTS

The project 'Shape our country' owes a substantive and financial debt to the Dutch Ministry of Agriculture, Nature and Food Quality, the Ministry of Transport, Public Works and Water Management, the Ministry of Housing, Spatial Planning and the Environment, the Directorate-General for Public Works and Water Management, Dutch Association of Regional Water Authorities and Leven met Water, Woning corporatie Ymere, MAB Development and Bouwfonds Ontwikkeling, BankGiro Loterij and ANWB. The project received substantive support from the following partners: Royal Institute of Dutch Architects (BNA), Dutch Professional Organisation of Urban Designers and Planners (BNSP), Netherlands Institute for planning and housing (Nirov), Chief government Architect, Routeontwerp, Friends of the Earth Netherlands (Milieudefensie), Habiforum and Kasteel Groeneveld.

The invitation to the Dutch public to 'Shape our country' was issued by the Netherlands Architecture Institute (NAI) for a period of six months from November 2008 to April 2009. For purposes of orientation the NAI indicated the headings under which planning assignments are usually gathered: mobility, housing, work, leisure, greenery and water.

The outcome of the project was a vast quantity of ideas and reactions that indicate that the familiar professional frames of references are becoming less relevant to the public in determining the direction of our spatial creativity. What does in fact motivate people is the enormous demand for solutions to major social issues. 'Shape our country' has demonstrated that the new spatial creativity starts with the pinpointing of an urgent issue and the ambition to do something about it rather than from a predetermined competence or specialization. The book *Architecture of Consequence* presents solutions to the public's problems.

'Shape our country' was the question; 'We make our country' is an answer. It is now a matter of putting the lessons into practice, doing what must be done and leaving aside what can be left.
NAI is the national platform for architecture, where challenges and designs can meet in the most inspiring way. 'Shape our country' is an explicit expression of the national debate and will be developed further as a programme. This book along with the new travelling exhibition which will open first at the São Paulo Biennale 2009 and is a follow-up to the project.

Instead of looking back on 'Shape our country' and offering a literal presentation of its harvest of ideas NAI has decided to produce a book geared to the future. Contemporary design practice has been scrutinized in the light of the project's conclusions, resulting in an agenda for spatial innovation to take architecture and environmental planning ahead in the next few years. There is a growing awareness that responding to the fundamental questions of our time is the responsibility of each and every one of us. The themes are universal; they stir and motivate the entire international community of architects. This book is a call to design a better world.

Countless creative individuals and socially aware organizations contributed to the project. They are already the shapers of our country. The 25 Dutch design practices given voice in this book are the first to follow. We are grateful for their astonishing work.